# Fresh Styles for Web Designers:

# Eye Candy from the Underground

**Curt Cloninger**

**New Riders** 201 West 103rd Street
Indianapolis, Indiana 46290

# Fresh Styles for Web Designers:
# Eye Candy from the Underground

## Trademarks

## Warning and Disclaimer

**Publisher**
David Dwyer

**Associate Publisher**
Al Valvano

**Executive Editor**
Karen Whitehouse

**Acquisitions Editor**
Michael Nolan

**Technical Editor**
Rafael Olivas

**Development Editor**
Victoria Elzey

**Product Marketing Manager**
Kathy Malmloff

**Managing Editor**
Sarah Kearns

**Project Editor**
Michael Thurston

**Copy Editor**
Gayle Johnson

**Cover and Interior Designer**
Carlos Segura

**Compositor**
Wil Cruz

**Indexer**
Lisa Stumpf

# Contents at a Glance

# Table of Contents

# contents

## contents

# contents

# Web Versus Print: A Note About URLs

The Web is an ever-changing flow of ideas, designs, and redesigns. Sites evolve and decay. Some move to new locations. Others disappear. By the time you read this book, some of the sites it describes will surely have changed, while others may have vanished altogether.

The medium's constant dynamism can wreak havoc on books about the web, and thus on those books' readers. You read about an interesting design or technological feat, fire up your web browser, and discover that the site no longer demonstrates what was discussed in the book.

Fortunately, you can often minimize the damage by bearing this in mind — if a particular web page seems to have disappeared, try factoring the URL to a simpler version. For instance, if **www.yahoo.com/games/ thrills/** no longer works, go back to its purest form, **www.yahoo.com/**, and see if you can navigate to the page's new location that way.

I will endeavor to keep the spirit of this book alive at **www.lab404.com/ dan/** with links to contemporary examples of these various styles. But if you're reading this book in 2010, the printed screen shots contained herein may well be your only link to a web that once was.

# About the Author

**Curt Cloninger** is a web designer, writer, and net artist. His commercial design portfolio includes sites like the award-winning (and revenue-generating) **integritymusic.com**. Curt is also a popular speaker at industry-wide internet conferences, and a regular contributor to design zines such as *A List Apart*. His net art has been exhibited at the Museum of Image and Sound in São Paulo, Brazil, archived on **rhizome.org**, and featured in digital art publications like *On/Off* and *Neural*. Curt lives at **lab404.com**, plays at **playdamage.org**, and continues to hold the heretical belief that beauty enhances usability.

# Dedication

For my dad. While other dads were playing golf at the country club, you were in the basement carving gnomes and lizards from gnarly chunks of driftwood. This book is partly your doing.

For Jesus, meta-creator. You laid the earth's cornerstone while the morning stars burst forth singing and the angels shouted for joy. You are my fire and my kerosene.

# Acknowledgments

Thanks to Joshua Davis, who started **dreamless.org** where I met Jeffrey Zeldman, who invited me to write an article for **alistapart.com** which was subsequently read by Michael Nolan, who then invited me to write this book. Thanks to all the people who had to endure crap while I wrote this book—particularly my wife Julie and my daughter Caroline. Thanks to Michael Nolan and Karen Whitehouse for letting this book be groovy. Thanks to Victoria Elzey and Rafael Olivas for keeping this book from becoming an all out freakfest. Thanks to Carlos Segura for designing such a beautifully unique, uniquely beautiful edition.

Mostly, respect to all the designers in this book for what you've contributed to the commercial web. May we all prove to be as passionate and ingenious.

"The Marshall guitar amplifier doesn't just get louder when you turn it up. It distorts the sound to produce a whole range of new harmonics, effectively turning a plucked string instrument into a bowed one. A responsible designer might try to overcome this limitation... But that sound became the sound of, among others, Jimi Hendrix. That sound is called 'electric guitar.'

...Since so much of our experience is mediated in some way or another, we have deep sensitivities to the signatures of different media. Artists play with these sensitivities, digesting the new and shifting the old. In the end, the characteristic forms of a tool's or medium's distortion, of its weakness and limitations, become sources of emotional meaning and intimacy."

—Brian Eno

Why begin a book about web design by quoting an ambient musician musing on the qualities of a guitar amplifier? First, because it's cool. Second, because from the very beginning, I want to make this point: The web is not broken, nor is it crippled, nor is it just waiting idly around for the advent of universal broadband so that it can magically morph into interactive television. Engaging and creative graphic design is happening on the web today—not in spite of its media characteristics, but because of them. Just as Jimi Hendrix was making creative music prior to the advent of the digital synthesizer, underground web designers are currently making creative sites prior to the advent of widespread broadband access. The trick lies in understanding the web as its own medium.

## Figure 01.01

*Marshall amplifiers*

# The Web Is Like... the Web

What are the web's unique attributes? Well, like a Marshall guitar amplifier (**Figure 01.01**), the web is not perfect. It has its creeping download rates and its browser incompatibilities. Users visit web sites with different screen sizes on different operating systems. These media "shortcomings" are best seen as opportunities to craft sites that take advantage of the web's uniqueness. But more often than not, these shortcomings are seen as barriers and hindrances to design. The reason is that most people still want the web to be print.

But the web is not print. Nor is the web television. The web is its own communications medium with its own media characteristics. When Jimi Hendrix first plugged his Stratocaster into a Marshall amp and cranked it up, he didn't say, "Hey, what's all

this distortion and coloration? That's not what my guitar is supposed to sound like!" To Hendrix, the Marshall amp didn't have shortcomings; it had personality. As a modern musician, Hendrix embraced the personality of his technology and incorporated it into his own unique musical style, and the face of modern music was changed forever. A new group of cutting-edge web designers are changing the face of the corporate web in the same way. These designers have embraced the warp and woof of the web on its own terms, and they are tweaking it and hacking it for all it's worth. The results are not only refreshing, but also very marketable.

The following pages cover 10 of these fresh, underground web design styles. I'll explore how they work and why they work. You'll learn some of the technical tricks that make these styles possible. I'll discuss which styles best apply to which particular commercial projects. (I'll even examine a style that has no practical commercial applications whatsoever!) Hopefully, by the time you're done, you will have broadened your skill set and design vocabulary, and you'll be rocking the medium yourself.

# The Problems: Legalism, Copycatting, and Print

I set out to write this book because graphic design on the corporate web is largely bland, passionless, and unengaging. The excuses offered are numerous: "Quality design is too difficult to achieve in all browsers on all platforms." "Our clients want their sites by yesterday, and we just don't have time to push the envelope." "We've already got these prefabricated templates, and they seem to work well enough." "Clients will buy anything we tell them, so why bust our chops developing something innovative and unique?" "After all, it's just the web."

As the web matures, these excuses won't cut it anymore. As soon as clients see that better web design work is possible, they won't settle for copycat sites. As soon as every company has a site that looks "as good as" **microsoft.com**, then what? As in print advertising (or TV, or radio, or any other form of advertising), the designers who can positively influence their target audiences within their given media are the designers who rise to the top.

Before I propose a solution to the current flavorlessness of the corporate web, let's examine how it came to be in such a bland state.

## Problem 1: The Usability Legalists

It is the constant mantra of today's usability expert that a site requires more than front-end style to succeed. A successful site requires consistent navigation, a logical hierarchy, well-written copy, efficient back-end programming, and a host of other commonsense components that have nothing to do with the whirling 3D letters of a 350K Flash splash page. These usability experts warn you repeatedly, "If a site has an elegant and appropriate design style but is unusable, it will fail."

I wholeheartedly agree! But allow me to propose the corollary: "If a site is perfectly usable but it lacks an elegant and appropriate design style, it will fail."

What happened was that Flash came along, and all these punk teen designers abandoned user-friendly interfaces to run amuck in a swamp of whirling polygonal irrelevance.

In opposition to these eccentric and bandwidth-hogging design extremes, the usability experts got together and basically dismissed creative web design *en toto*. They then proceeded to declare rigorous site-building "laws," some of which read like dictatorial edicts rather than the mere "guidelines" they purport to be. (For example: "About 99% of the time, the presence of Flash on a web site constitutes a usability disease." —Jakob Nielsen) In short, the usability gurus have thrown out the baby of creative web design with the bath water of bad, self-indulgent web design. Such careful avoidance of "bad usability" at all costs has fostered an entire generation of safe, bland, copycat web sites that are about as engaging as a book on usability testing methodologies.

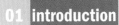

Admittedly, creative graphic design is not the panacea to every ailing web site. It still takes meaty copy, a logical navigation scheme, and a well-considered architecture to make a successful site. Above all, it takes a focused narrative voice—an angle, a plan, a consistent point of view—to unify a site's disparate elements and give it a cohesive personality. I simply want to declare that creative visual design is an integral part of this overall site-building mix. To dismiss front-end design as mere "icing" is to jeopardize the success of any site.

## Problem 2: The "One Size Fits All" Syndrome

A sort of copycat mentality has plagued commercial web design from the beginning, as if the web is only big enough for a few basic types of sites. The logic goes like this: "Why reinvent the web design wheel when sites like microsoft.com, **ibm.com**, **msnbc.com**, and even **yahoo.com** have proven successful? Why not just imitate the few highly visible, frequently visited sites on the web?" Clients are pleased because they get a site that looks familiar. Designers pat themselves on the back because they've mastered that professional, muted-blue, left-hand navigation bar, close-cropped, tri-tone, stock photography look. And suddenly, the entire commercial web looks more or less identical.

So what's the problem? If the visitors are happy, they're happy. The problem is, the visitors aren't happy. People visit microsoft.com not because it's well-designed, but because they have to—because their software just crashed again. I propose that if microsoft.com and **compaq.com** switched front-end design styles, the traffic to those two sites would remain relatively unaltered (**Figures 01.02 and 01.03**).

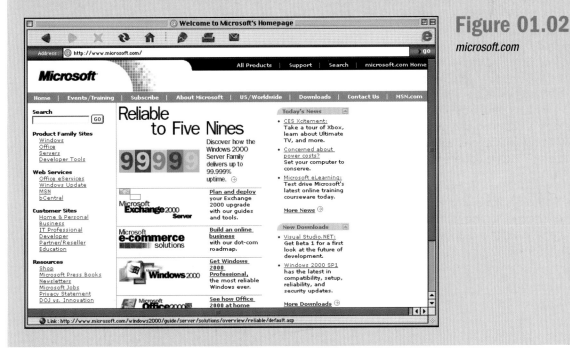

# Figure 01.02

*microsoft.com*

**Figure 01.03**

*compaq.com*

True, there are sites like yahoo.com and **amazon.com** that do succeed in part due to the merits of their design. But not every site is a search engine (actually, few are), and not every site is a kitchen sink online e-tailer (actually, few are). So, if you're building a marketing site for a local bowling alley, why on earth would you make it look like yahoo.com?

Granted, yahoo.com is heavily trafficked, it downloads quickly, and it's supposedly easy to use. Personally, I don't find Yahoo! all that easy to use, but let's just assume for the sake of argument that Yahoo! is the epitome of user-friendly search engine design. So what? Are navigable topical indices of primary importance for a bowling alley site? Is a three-second download time really important enough to cause a bowling alley site to entirely abandon the use of jpeg images? No.

Not every site is an e-commerce site. Not every site is an online newsmagazine. Not every site is a search engine. A Vespa Scooter is a terrific city vehicle, but you wouldn't take it off-road (**Figure 01.04**). To go off-road, you need a sturdy vehicle of the four-wheel variety (**Figure 01.05**). Similarly, amazon.com sports a terrific all-purpose e-commerce design, but would you use that same design at **pepsi.com**? Different jobs require different styles—hence the need for a broader, more diverse web design vocabulary.

**Figure 01.04**
*Vespa Scooter*

**Figure 01.05**
*Polaris four-wheeler*

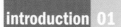

## Problem 3: The Virus of Print Design

Have you ever stopped to think about how ibm.com got to look like ibm.com in the first place? Follow me if you will. IBM has an ongoing relationship with a big-client marketing firm. This big-client marketing firm is primarily trained in print design. The web emerges as a medium, and IBM asks its print-centric marketing firm to design IBM's corporate web site. So the print-centric marketing firm proceeds to port a bunch of its already-created IBM print advertising (stock photos, catalog copy) to the web, and presto!—a bland corporate web presence is born.

"But they must know what they're doing; they're IBM!" And so you copy ibm.com, other designers copy you, and the virus of print design is disseminated throughout the corporate web.

# The Solution: Personal Passion

Why reinvent the web design wheel? Because the web design wheel has actually yet to be invented. There's nothing inherently superior or intuitive or *a priori* about the current design face of the commercial web. The commercial web doesn't have to look the way it does. Indeed, there are several very compelling reasons for it to look totally other than the way it does. With thousands of different companies representing thousands of different products and services, why should the commercial web look so homogenous?

Early television was basically just radio with the addition of TV cameras in the radio studio. It took television producers a while to figure out that an announcer standing next to a new Maytag washing machine did *not* have to say, "Hi, I'm here standing next to this new Maytag washing machine." How long did it take web designers to figure out that links need not be indicated by the words "click here"?

In order to move beyond a conservative, copycat style, you must look beyond the inbred corporate web to the personal sites of today's leading web designers. When they're not working their day jobs, most top-notch web designers are pushing the web design envelope after-hours on their own personal sites—manipulating current technologies and expanding the medium's design vocabulary. Many leading-edge web design firms are using their own portfolio sites to experiment in similar ways.

Fortunately for us, most of the hacks, techniques, and styles pioneered on these personal sites eventually find their way into commercial sites. So you don't have to sit around thinking, "Sure, this stuff looks cool, but how can I incorporate these techniques into an actual commercial project?" All of these styles have already been successfully incorporated into actual commercial projects. So, in addition to pure, "for-passion" sites, you'll see plenty of commercial sites as proofs of concept.

In order to avoid the drones, sometimes you have to leave the hive. All 10 of the design styles discussed in this book sprang from a dissatisfaction with the status quo, a love of the web as a medium, and a passion for evocative, communicative design. Many of these sites were meticulously and laboriously crafted with no expectation of monetary remuneration whatsoever. All of these sites are sites of passion. Hopefully they will infuse you with a similar love for what you do and a desire to design more creatively.

Ultimately, people (yes, even customers) are moved by what they feel. All truly successful human communication touches people not just in their minds, but in their entire beings—body, soul, and spirit. Yes, visitors have to be able to use your sites. But visitors should also be able to feel your sites. The web is not a database. The web is a communications medium. These 10 underground styles aren't magic. They are merely vehicles that you can use to break out of the monotony of today's safe, commercial web.

Yes, it is possible to communicate a meaningful and engaging human experience over the web, even at 56K. You need only look to Sir Hendrix, Master of the Marshall (**Figure 01.06**), who saw potential where others saw only shortcomings. May your own design work be similarly enlightened as you proceed to rock this strange hybrid medium called the web.

**Figure 01.06**
*Jimi Hendrix*

"Glory be to God for dappled things—
For skies of couple-color as a brinded cow;
For rose-moles all in stipple upon trout
  that swim;
Fresh-firecoal chestnut-falls; finches' wings;
Landscape plotted and pieced—fold, fallow
  and plow;
And all trades, their gear and tackle
  and trim.

All things counter, original, spare, strange;
Whatever is fickle, freckled (who knows how?)
With swift, slow; sweet, sour; adazzle, dim;
He fathers-forth whose beauty is past change:
Praise him."

—Gerald Manley Hopkins

Web sites aren't made by computers; web sites are made by people. This fact is easily forgotten by today's web designers, because very little about a web site is physical. Web pages are rarely printed, digital stock photography is often employed, and most web design tools are just pieces of software. It is not at all unusual for entire web sites to be created and deployed without importing any analog media. From wireframe mock-ups through site development to the "go live" event, the entire web design process is often entirely self-contained within the confines of the machine. OK, maybe you made a rough sketch on a napkin during an after-hours brainstorming session, or maybe you drew a vague site map on a white board during a development meeting. But many site-building projects never cross the digital divide.

And yet the physical world in which we all live exists outside the computer. A dry leaf crunches underfoot, an oak tree gnarls and twists, water glistens and beads, a face scrunches and contorts. These vivid sensory experiences cannot be reproduced on a web site using HTML text and grayscale stock photography. To create a web site that feels like real life, you've got to intentionally import design elements from real life. Not every line in real life is parallel or perpendicular. Not every surface is evenly shaded. Not every object is perfectly rectangular. In real life, shapes might be symmetrical, but more often than not, they have irregular outlines. The real world is less Cubist and more Baroque.

The design style that best manages to distill the chaos of the world into bits is the Gothic Organic Style (**Figure 02.01**). Gothic organic designers are not photorealists. The idea is not to fully represent every single aspect of the real world on a web site. That would be impossible (not to mention bandwidth-hogging). Instead, gothic organicists take a more abstract "part for the whole" design approach that suggests and connotes the irregularities and entropies of real life without literally depicting all of them. By using the right combination of representative real-world textures, shapes, and images, these designers can conjure up a believable (or at least enjoyable) analog experience.

**Figure 02.01**

*entropy8.com*

The Gothic Organic Style is "organic" in that it uses human forms, plant forms, and other organic shapes and textures as its building blocks. In that sense, gothic organicism differs greatly from many of the other styles in this book, which are more geometric and "straight-angled" in origin and nature.

The Gothic Organic Style is "gothic" for two reasons. First, like the Gothic architecture that birthed the early cathedrals, gothic organicism is intricate, billowing, overblown, and all-encompassing. It is less like the World Trade Center and more like the Cathedral of Notre Dame. A more contemporary architectural comparison is between the two Guggenheims—New York versus Bilbao. The original New York Guggenheim (**Figure 02.02**) was patterned after circular geometrical shapes (I'm grossly oversimplifying). It's more akin to the tight, grid-based icon style I'll examine later. The Bilbao Guggenheim (**Figure 02.03**) was patterned after, well, a fish. It doesn't get any more gothic organic than a fish.

**Figure 02.02**
*New York Guggenheim*

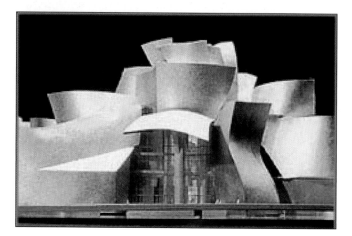

**Figure 02.03**
*Bilbao Guggenheim*

The second reason for the "gothic" name is slightly less scholastic. The pioneering practitioner of gothic organicism, Aurelia Harvey, owes a debt to the contemporary underground "gothic" scene—death rock, black clothing, self-mutilating performance art, and the like. Hence the interest in cadavers, decay, and, most noticeably, dark backgrounds. But your applications of this style probably won't be as spooky as all that.

Because the Gothic Organic Style is ultimately sense-engaging, it is most applicable for branding or product-enhancement sites. Have you been hired to do the promotional site for a new album or film? Are your clients looking to create an experience that leads fans to explore the themes and ideas beneath the project's surface? Then gothic organic design is a logical approach. Granted, not everyone gets hired to make such sites, and not every musical artist has a story behind the song. Still, an increasing number of nonweb media entertainment companies are using the web less as a place for frequently asked questions and more as yet another way to brand their projects. In a sense, these branding web sites become like CD covers or movie trailers—just more interactive and thus more engaging.

Other possible commercial applications for this style include sports sites, trekking/tour sites, cruise ship sites, and any site that seeks to create a "you are here" immersive environment. Rather than small jpeg snapshots of what your white-water rafting experience looks like, better than even a five-second, thumbnail-sized QuickTime film of a run through the rapids, why not an entire screen-covering page that makes you feel like you're in the raft? The background layer could be an abstract animated gif that gives you the feeling of rocks and water overhead. Ambient audio of rapids and excited yelling could fade in and out. The QuickTime movies and jpeg snapshots could still be used as insets within this design, but if you want to put your visitor in the midst of the action, why just give him a tiny window into the experience and ask him to trust you for the rest? The web is far more powerful than a printed brochure. Why continue to waste its strengths on mere brochure-ware?

The keys to gothic organic design are deciding which elements of "real life" best represent a "real-life" web experience and deciding how to render those elements most effectively given the limitations of the web as a medium. Hopefully, after you examine some master sites and discover some practical design techniques, you'll be comfortable enough with gothic organicism to begin incorporating it into some of your projects.

# Case Studies

If it weren't for sculptor/web designer Aurelia Harvey, I wouldn't be writing this chapter. She is single-handedly responsible for crafting gothic organicism (although she would have never called it that), for advancing its online design vocabulary, and even for discovering and developing its commercial applications. There are other design schools in this book for which a single person is solely responsible (Lo-Fi Grunge, 1950s Hello Kitty), but none are so closely associated with their pioneers as gothic organicism is with Harvey.

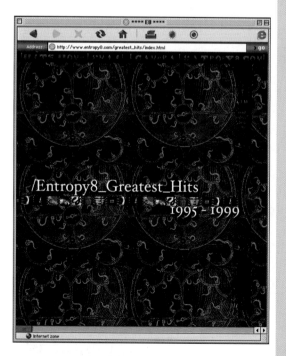

## Figure 02.04

*entropy8.com*

# Symmetry Is Death: Entropy8

In 1995, when few people were even aware of the web, Harvey was already experimenting with unorthodox HTML, animation, and visual narrative. Her primary vehicle of experimentation was her personal site, **entropy8.com** (**Figure 02.04**). Harvey has since merged with Michael Sämyn to form **entropy8zuper.org**. Their current experiments in real-time visual collaboration, although mind-blowing, are beyond the scope of this book. So keep in mind that this is someone's "old" work—work that she has outgrown but that still amazes and instructs, even by contemporary web design standards.

Harvey says, "Art is for all the things you can't say out loud." So entropy8.com is first and foremost a means of personal visual expression. As such, some of its navigation is difficult, some of its meaning is cryptic, and some of its images are hard to swallow. But if you wade with me through this world for a while, you'll come away with some useful web design approaches—approaches that Harvey herself has applied successfully to her own commercial gigs.

The first striking thing about Entropy8 is its mystery and allure. Images are distinguishable, but just barely. The idea is to create a sense of seduction and curiosity that lead to surfer exploration and involvement. For instance, the navigation menu presents a series of highly textured, closely cropped images (**Figure 02.05**). The only image that has any sort of explanation at all is the WORK! image.

**Figure 02.05**

*entropy8.com*

The top-left image on the menu is vaguely squidlike. Clicking it leads to an expanded page with tentacles in the background (**Figure 02.06**). Note that the tentacles are still primarily decorative, more suggestive than overt. The tentacles connote fern fronds, plant tendrils, fractal spirals, and other growing things expanding organically into the void—all obeying entropy, the tendency of any ordered system to head toward chaos. Tentacles also represent the linked nature of the web, where a central source reaches out in several different directions at once. And how many tentacles does an octopus have? Hence Entropy8.

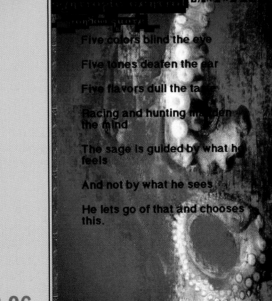

**Figure 02.06**

*entropy8.com*

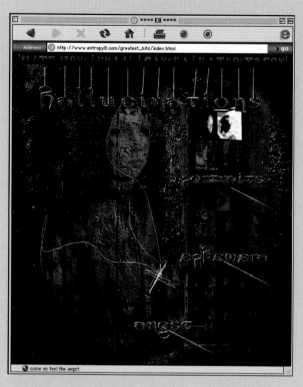

**Figure 02.07**

*entropy8.com*

Whether or not you "get" this metaphorical picture language, there's no mistaking the feeling that you are in exotic web territory. Entropy8 is no ordinary "click here" site. The sense of vague implicit meaning either propels you to drill deeper or causes you to bail out in search of more didactic pastures. Thus, gothic organicism is not the optimal style for a data-centric site like **usatoday.com**. But not every site is an online newspaper.

Entropy8 was built back when 640×480 was still the default window size. Hence, Harvey's pages are none too liquid. They are mostly scrunched into the top-left corner of the browser window. When Entropy8 was actively maintained, there was a brief instructional arrow at the site's entrance, asking visitors to resize their browser

windows accordingly. You can achieve the same resizing effect sans instructions by simply "centering" the active area using border frames and percentage widths. (I examine this solution later in the "Controlled Window Sizes" section.)

You can do certain tricks with background images when a surfer's window size is known and controlled. Such tricks simply aren't possible when the surfer's window size is unknown and variable. If I know that someone's browser window is at most 480 pixels wide, I can build a detailed background image that begins scrolling sideways at 490 pixels without worrying about it. Otherwise, I have to build my background image to accommodate the possibility of a 1280-pixel-wide screen while still allowing for the possibility of a 480-pixel-wide screen.

## Figure 02.08

*entropy8.com*

Such a large image, in order to load in a decent amount of time, has to be less detailed. And it must look good cropped width-wise at 480, 800, 1024, and so on. When the browser's window size is controlled, such considerations need no longer limit you.

I explore other ways to get around the background image/window size problem in subsequent chapters, but Harvey's solution of limiting the window size works best for her backgrounds, which are necessarily detailed and thus are too slow-loading to be created at 1280×1024 pixels. Why spend so much energy worrying about background images? Because for Harvey's particular brand of gothic organicism, background images are crucial.

Harvey's background images are the primal swamp from which her text and foreground images emerge (**Figure 02.07**). These backgrounds are dark, intricate, large, and fraught with all sorts of "real-world" gunk—veins, fractures, creases, smudges, and other sundry evidence of decay. In other words, these backgrounds are highly, realisti-cally textured. Some of these backgrounds are photographs of textured real-world objects. Other backgrounds appear to be scanned images of mixed-media analog art collages (**Figure 02.08**). Many backgrounds have been further tweaked and manipulated in Photoshop using a combination of lighting effects and layer masks (**Figure 02.09**).

**Figure 02.09**

*entropy8.com*

As soon as the browser's window size has been controlled and the background images have been made to fill the entire window, Harvey can then begin to accurately position foreground images over these backgrounds (**Figure 02.07**). She achieves this near-exact positioning of foreground elements using a combination of tables and transparent spacer gifs, as was the technique in those post-Siegel, pre-Cascading Style Sheets days. (The same positioning can better be achieved these days using Cascading Style Sheets.) Harvey's backgrounds as such act less like repeating textile patterns and more like actual elements of the overall page design.

Harvey further ups the ante by making many of her foreground images transparent and animated (via either DHTML or gif animation). The results are very unweblike. On one page, a giant angsty wire contraption lashes out repeatedly into the decaying void (**Figure 02.07**). On another page, a geisha girl dances elegantly above stylized tessellating globes (**Figure 02.10**). On yet another page, gold-encrusted letters float surrealistically over yet another squidlike background (**Figure 02.08**). What all these foreground images abhor and lack is a rectangular boundary. Yes, all web images have to be more or less square. But if you use transparent gifs, these square borders need not show. Thus, you have moving images and shapes that seem to possess their own edges and weight, floating above backgrounds that seem to possess their own history and texture. Just like in the real world.

## Figure 02.10

*entropy8.com*

# Chaos Does Commerce: Conscience Records

Throughout this book, my job is to consistently and convincingly answer the ever-present objection, "Sure, that works on an artsy personal home page, but what about a commercial site?" Can the Gothic Organic Style be used successfully in a commercial setting? Definitely. The first shining example of this is Conscience Records (**Figure 02.11**). Built by Entropy8 in 1996 to feature the bands of an underground record label, **conscience.com** still appeals today. All Harvey's signature techniques are present. The navigational "home" button is a transparent animated gif of a rotating brain. The backgrounds are all glowing red, scored with filamented black textures. Harvey uses the same unorthodox combination of flowing cursive arabesque fonts and distressed grunge fonts.

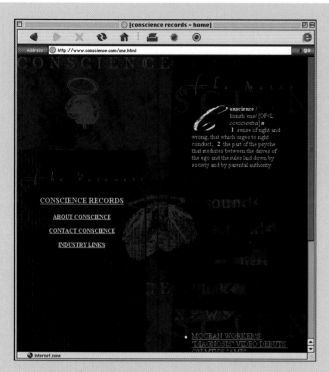

## Figure 02.11

*conscience.com*

The one thing present here that is lacking at Entropy8 is a semi-straightforward navigation scheme. True, conscience.com probably won't win any awards for most hierarchically consistent site, but it's plenty navigable. In the "bands" and "music" sections, Harvey even uses an efficient combination of frames and pull-down menus to walk you through the various artists while still leaving the main navigation elements in view (**Figure 02.12**). Ultimately, however, the Gothic Organic Style can be implemented apart from this particular site hierarchy. There's nothing inherently wedding the two.

Even at a commercial site—with its obligatory navigation menu, HTML text, and products to display—Harvey chooses to view the entire browser window as a work of art. The navigation elements are not extraneous or relegated to a corner. They are front and center, acting as part of the overall design (**Figure 02.11**). conscience.com is not space-stingy. Plenty of negative space does nothing but radiate red and look funky. And yet the text is not cramped, set apart as it is from the rest of the design by its own left and right "gutters" of negative space. Thus, the presentation of information is not hindered.

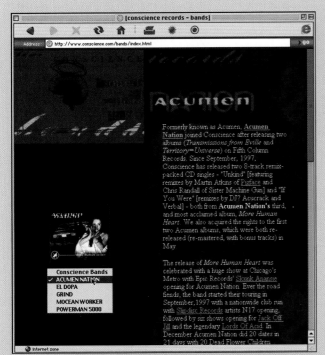

## Figure 02.12
*conscience.com*

Usability extremists might argue that this design distracts from the overall goal of the site. But what is the goal of this site, really? Is the goal that every surfer be able to immediately access the statistic "El Dopa's first release was the 1995 seven-song EP *Hindu Freak Love*"? Or is the goal of this site that every surfer leave thinking, "That site is hip; those bands are hip; I'm hip. Gotta get my hands on that *Hindu Freak Love* EP"? When the goal of the site is product branding, setting a mood becomes more important than immaculate usability.

I've been surfing since conscience.com first went live, and I've yet to come across a site quite like it. Is there a market for unique, outstanding, never-before-seen sites? Sure there is. Any company with a unique, out-standing, never-before-seen product—that's your market. In the case of Conscience Records, Harvey's particular style happens to perfectly fit these particular bands (she's even designed some of their album covers). But can the Gothic Organic Style be adapted to fit the needs of a more mainstream pop artist? Is Janet Jackson mainstream enough for you?

# Behind the Velvet Rope: Janet Jackson

Janet Jackson's Velvet Rope site (another Entropy8 creation) is more boxy than some of Harvey's earlier work, but the textured backgrounds and crisp, irregularly shaped foreground images still manage to give this site that signature gothic organic look (**Figure 02.13**). Harvey is up to her old tricks, using cryptic navigation elements once again. Tiny, closely cropped image squares throughout the site act as alluring link invitations (**Figure 02.14**). There is also a text navigation menu at the top for those more verbally inclined. This time, Harvey and cohort Marc Antony Vose overcome the window size problem a bit more elegantly by centering the entire site within a 750×360 pixel frame. The surrounding frames simply form a black border that shrinks or expands depending on the browser's window size.

The Velvet Rope site seeks to create a "story behind the album" experience. As a surfer, you become a detective, invited to explore and discover the hidden meanings and motivations "behind the velvet rope." Disappointingly, the answers usually come in the form of insipid Janet sound bites or trite behind-the-scenes photo-shoot footage.

Yet none of this pseudo-profundity is Harvey's fault. You can only work with what you're given. The real fun of this site is its design—the lush backgrounds (**Figure 02.15**), the then-innovative JavaScript and Shockwave rollovers, and the creative use of frames to present multimedia content (**Figure 02.16**). Most impressive is the feeling that you are looking into a worn wooden box of someone's personal memorabilia, rather than merely staring at light on a screen. This site makes me want to buy *The Velvet Rope,* and I don't even like Janet Jackson. (OK, so her "Rhythm Nation" video does happen to rock my world. But it's a guilty pleasure at best.)

If Entropy8 can make Janet Jackson seem profound, gothic organicism can surely add some depth and dimension to your next applicable project. Again, this style need not be applied 100%. It may be admixed, toned down, modified, and even trashed. The point is to take what you can use and leave the rest. I'm not trying to make you pierce your nipple and go on tour with Nine Inch Nails. I am merely adding another set of tools to your web design arsenal.

# Figure 02.13
*Janet: The Velvet Rope*

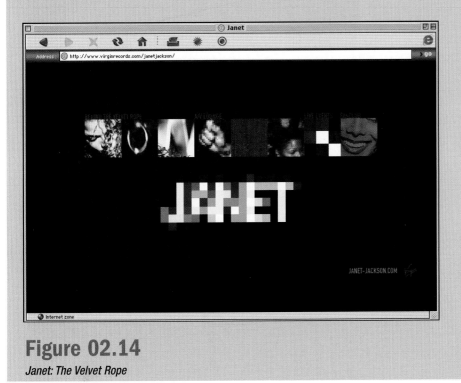

# Figure 02.14
*Janet: The Velvet Rope*

## Figure 02.15

*Janet: The Velvet Rope*

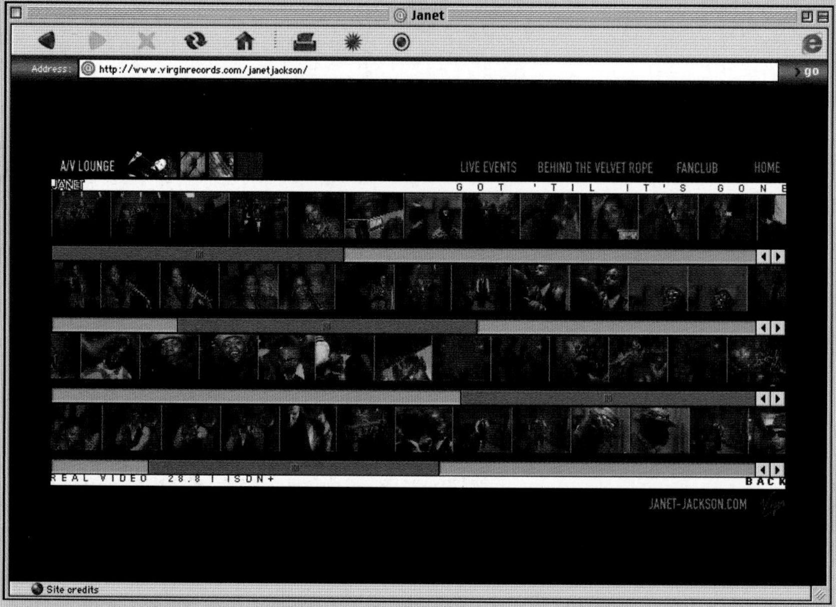

## Figure 02.16

*Janet: The Velvet Rope*

# Techniques

As with some other styles in this book, much of the "art" of gothic organicism is just that—the ability to create beautiful art. I can't teach you how to create beautiful art in half a chapter. But I can point you in some specific techniques that you'll need to know in order to make your own gothic organic sites.

# Analogesque Background Textures

The goal of gothic organicism is to come up with textures and images *that don't look digital*. It helps to start with objects in the real world that have some wear on them. A macro lens for your camera is a plus. Get so close that the objects themselves become indistinguishable. In other words, stop taking pictures of objects, and begin taking pictures of textures—the veins of a leaf, flaking paint, the psychedelic swirl of spilled oil.

To further "age" your pictures, print them, physically crumple them, and then scan the crumpled print. Or write on your prints. Or scar them. Or apply any number of other analog collage techniques that designers practiced before there were computers. This analog "tweak" phase adds a bit of real-world "wear" to your images prior to their journey into the machine.

Then, in Photoshop, use noise filters and other filters to get a grainy, worn look. Experiment with duotone and tritone treatments. If you add the proper amount of visual noise, a duotone image can start to look antique. If HTML text needs to appear on top of your backgrounds, take care to leave some negative space for that to happen.

Harvey herself suggests keeping a texture library. **Figure 02.17** shows a tile she made early in her web design career by experimenting in Corel Painter. She confesses to having used this same single texture as a base element in numerous pages. Her advice is to mess around in an image-generation program, keeping an eye open for interesting developments while being mindful not to go overboard and muddy everything up. When you come across a texture worth keeping, archive it and use it.

## Figure 02.17

*Entropy8 texture*

Although most of Harvey's backgrounds are large and not meant to "tile," she does sometimes use tiny background images that tile repeatedly, causing a seamless texture effect (**Figure 02.18**). Creating such seamless tiling backgrounds is relatively straightforward.

Start with a tiny square image of the texture you want to tile. Let's assume your image is 90×90 pixels. In Adobe Photoshop, under Filters/Others, open the Offset filter. Under Undefined Areas, choose Wrap Around. And then, in the Horizontal and Vertical fields, enter half the dimensions of your image (in this case, you would enter 45 and 45). Click OK.

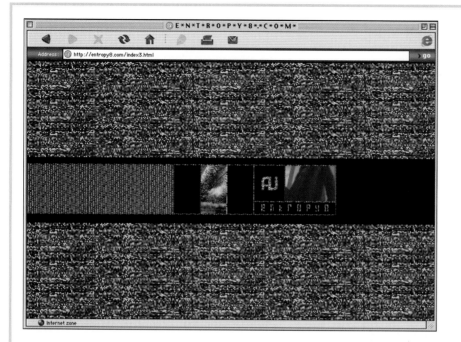

## Figure 02.18

*entropy8.com*

There should now be two objectionable lines on your image, one running down the middle horizontally and the other running down the middle vertically. Choose the rubber stamp tool from the Tools menu. You will "lift" some texture from near the line and "stamp" it on the line. To lift the desired texture, put the stamp tool over the area you want to lift, hold down the Alt (on the Mac, Option) key, and click. To stamp that texture, put the stamp tool on the line and click.

This is a hack, so just keep at it until the lines seem to disappear. You might have to lift a bit from one side of the line and stamp and then lift a bit from the other side of the line and stamp, but eventually you should get it. Save this 90×90 image as a gif or jpeg, call it into your page as a background image, and observe. If the seams are still too obvious, return to Photoshop and repeat until seamlessness is achieved.

# Foreground Images with Irregular Borders

The secret of irregular image borders is choosing organic shapes that are unboxy and then saving them as transparent gifs, properly anti-aliased to blend with your page's predominant background color. For photographs, do the following in Photoshop:

1. Create your textured background image.

2. Using the eyedropper tool, select the predominant color of your textured background image.

3. Open your foreground image.

4. Using the paint bucket tool (configured with some amount of tolerance), fill in the background area of your foreground image with the color you've selected. Keep "pouring" the color until you've masked the background area as much as possible. Use the magic wand tool (configured with the necessary amount of tolerance) to isolate and select problem chunks of the background if necessary. When you're finished, the isolated foreground object should be the only thing not masked.

5. Using the magic eraser tool, click the background color you've been dumping. This makes it transparent.

6. Save your foreground image as a transparent gif.

There are more elaborate ways to do this involving paths and layers, but you get the idea. As soon as your foreground objects integrate unobjectionably with your (preferably dark) background textures, you are on your way to gothic organic Jedi-dom.

Whereas most web sites strive for noonday crispness, gothic organic sites often seek the gray and murky in-betweens. **greyscale.net** is a classic example of this shadowy, underwater world, replete with all sorts of writhing organic foreground entities (**Figure 02.19**). Unlike Entropy8, Greyscale often opts for totally black backgrounds. This lack of background texture focuses all the attention on the foreground images. Greyscale's foreground plant/machine/ animal amalgams are skillfully created using 3D modeling software, giving Greyscale a more animated, futuristic look versus Entropy8's photographic, neo-Victorian look.

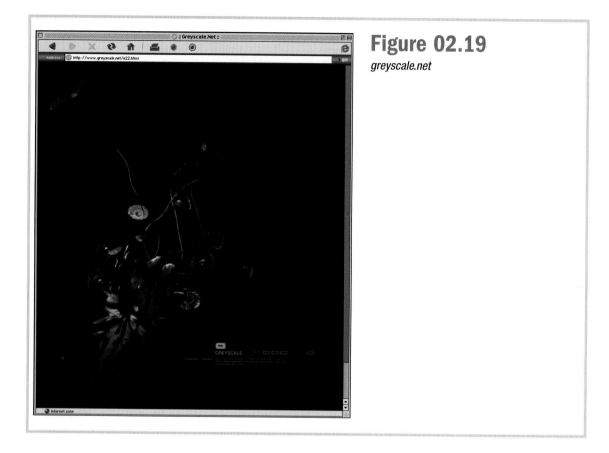

## Figure 02.19
*greyscale.net*

# Transparent Animated Gifs

The only thing more eye-catching than a transparent gif on a textured background is a transparent *animated* gif on a textured background. But first, a word of caution: As with all web animation (Flash, DHTML, QuickTime, whatever), use gif animation wisely and sparingly. Nothing draws inordinate attention to itself in the browser window quite like motion.

That said, Harvey's dancing geisha girl and her angst whip are wonderful examples of bold, attention-demanding animation for animation's sake. In contrast, her rotating brain (**Figure 02.20**) is an excellent use of animation as a navigational element. Were the brain not rotating, you would lose it in the noise of the page. But because it is rotating, it assumes the prominence that a "home" button should have, despite its smaller size and its inconsistent visual manifestations from page to page.

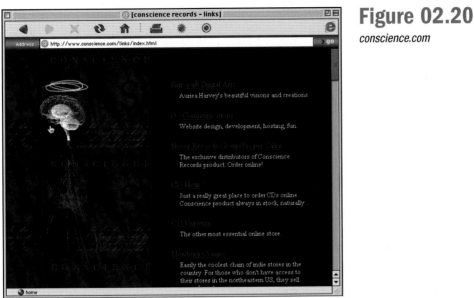

**Figure 02.20**

*conscience.com*

Regardless of which gif animation program you use, you still need to make your gif transparent, just as you made your other foreground images transparent. (You might even have to add transparency frame by frame.)

When creating your animations, make sure that your "focus object" (dancing girl, whip, whatever) doesn't ever abut or leave the edges of your gif. Otherwise, when you make the gif's background transparent, your focus object will seem to disappear behind the invisible edges of your overall gif, thus making the boxy outline of your gif visible by inference (**Figure 02.21**). You want your focus object to appear unbounded. It should seem to merely exist on the page, able to move about as it pleases (**Figure 02.22**).

**Figure 02.21**

*Incorrect (edge showing)*

**Figure 02.22**

*Correct (no edge showing)*

# Controlled Window Sizes

As promised, here is the "centering" nested frameset hack from the Janet Jackson site. All content resides in the "main" frame, which in this case is 750 pixels wide by 360 pixels high. The main frame is centered in the browser window, surrounded on all sides by empty black frames (**Figure 02.13**). The main frame automatically becomes scrollable when the surfer's window is less than 750×360. This nested frameset solution affords all the background image control required by gothic organicism without having to resort to the sometimes-objectionable JavaScript pop-up window.

The following code shows the main HTML frameset page that calls in the rest of the subpages. **Zblack.html** is just a blank page with its background color set to black (**<body bgcolor="000000">**). Note that it is called in four separate times in order to surround the main frame. The subpage **main.html** is the centered page that contains the actual content.

```
<html>
<head>
<title>Janet</title>
</head>

<FRAMESET ROWS="*,360,*" FRAMESPACING="0" FRAMEBORDER="no" BORDER="0">

        <FRAME NAME="top"
                SRC="Zblack.html"
                MARGINHEIGHT="0"
                MARGINWIDTH="0"
                SCROLLING="no"
                NORESIZE>

        <FRAMESET COLS="*,750,*" BORDER="0" FRAMEBORDER="no" FRAMESPACING="0">

                <FRAME NAME="1"
                        SRC="Zblack.html"
                        MARGINHEIGHT="0"
                        MARGINWIDTH="0"
                        SCROLLING="no"
                        NORESIZE>

                <FRAME NAME="main"
                        SRC="main.html"
                        MARGINHEIGHT="0"
                        MARGINWIDTH="0"
                        SCROLLING="auto"
                        NORESIZE>

                <FRAME NAME="2"
                        SRC="Zblack.html"
                        MARGINHEIGHT="0"
                        MARGINWIDTH="0"
                        SCROLLING="no"
                        NORESIZE>

        </FRAMESET>

        <FRAME NAME="bottom"
                SRC="Zblack.html"
                MARGINHEIGHT="0"
                MARGINWIDTH="0"
                SCROLLING="no"
                NORESIZE>

</FRAMESET>
</html>
```

# Intentional Exploitation of Vertical Scrolling

Many gothic organic designers intentionally design their pages to scroll vertically. Most corporate design is intent on having as much information as possible crammed "above the fold" in the pre-scrolled window that the site visitor sees initially. Yet at this point in the web's development, vertical scrolling is a normal part of surfing. Even the novice web user knows he probably has to scroll some to get to the bottom of a page.

With this in mind, why not have some fun with vertical scrolling? Why not build long pages and design them in a way that visually invites the visitor to scroll down? After you've eliminated horizontal background tiling by controlling the width of the viewable browser window, vertical tiling of a large background image need not be problematic.

As soon as your foreground layout "ends," the browser window stops scrolling. So one way to keep your large background images from scrolling vertically is to make them tall enough to fill even the largest monitor (1000 pixels high should reasonably do it) and then design your foreground layout not to exceed the height of your background image. This ensures that your window ends before your background image begins to tile (**Figure 02.23**).

Notice that in **Figure 02.23** the vertically hanging foreground elements tell the surfer, "You haven't seen it all; there's more down below." Harvey is not trying to fit all of her best design "above the fold." Instead, she makes sure that this doesn't happen so that the viewer knows to scroll down. The same is true of this screen at greyscale.net (**Figure 02.24**). The focus object begins halfway down the viewable window and continues off the bottom of it. There are no links above the fold. The surfer is forced to scroll in order to find the link that leads to the next page. Such "forced" scrolling might be a bit extreme for a commercial site, but it does force the surfer to explore and thus become more involved.

**Figure 02.23**

*entropy8.com*

**Figure 02.24**

*greyscale.net*

Gothic organicism is not for Yahoo! or MSNBC, but regardless of what many novice surfers
might initially think, there are more sites on the commercial web than Yahoo! and MSNBC.
For clients who want an immersive web environment experientially analogous to the real world,
these gothic organic approaches might be just the ticket.

# Sites Mentioned in This Chapter

http://www.entropy8.com/
greatest_hits/index.html

http://www.entropy8zuper.org

http://www.conscience.com

Janet Jackson's Velvet Rope
site is no longer viewable at
http://www.virgin records.com/
janetjackson, but can still
be accessed from
http://www.lab404.com/janet

http://www.greyscale.net

"There are better ways to portray spirits and essences than to get them all tangled up with statistical graphics."

—Edward Tufte

"We need body rockin, not perfection. Lemme get some action from the back section."

—Beastie Boys

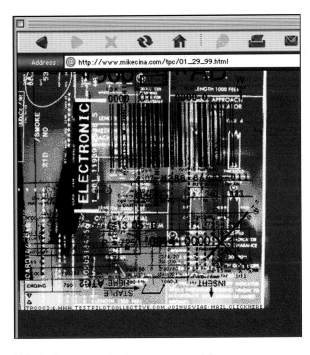

**Figure 03.01**

*testpilotcollective.com*

What do you get when you combine a respect for Bauhaus design; a fetish for maps, charts, and graphs; and a desire to exploit the limitations of the web for fun and profit? Answer: The Grid-Based Icon Style of web design. In the early days of the web, a house DJ named Mike Cina began applying his aesthetic sensibilities to digital typography. Eventually, Cina and cohorts Matt Desmond and Joseph Kral combined forces to form the digital foundry known as Test Pilot Collective. Their fonts were meticulous and fresh, often sporting a stylized, pixelated look that was perfect for the web. But what caught the attention of the underground web design community more than anything was their insanely creative splash pages.

Every day for nearly two years now, **testpilotcollective.com** has sported a new splash page. The early splash pages were often little more than scanned analog "chartjunk"—airline tickets, bar codes, population statistics, and other "found" objects (**Figure 03.01**). At first glance, these splashes seem officious and meaningful, but further examination reveals a more playful, tongue-in-cheek intent. True to his DJ roots, Cina was remixing source material to develop his own fresh style.

Mike Cina is an admitted fan of Edward Tufte's classic *The Visual Display of Quantitative Information,* but Tufte himself likely would not have approved of Test Pilot Collective's "ready-made" design methods. Whereas Tufte stressed removing extraneous design in order to reveal only the pertinent information in statistical charts, TPC stressed exploiting the noninformational abstract beauty of charts for pure aesthetic pleasure.

Gradually, the Test Pilot Collective splashes began to include more and more unscanned "original" designs, abstract line art layouts created in Illustrator or Photoshop to replicate the vibe of the analog charts and graphs so dear to the hearts of Cina and company. These new splashes began to look more like architectural blueprints, or simply abstract geometric shapes.

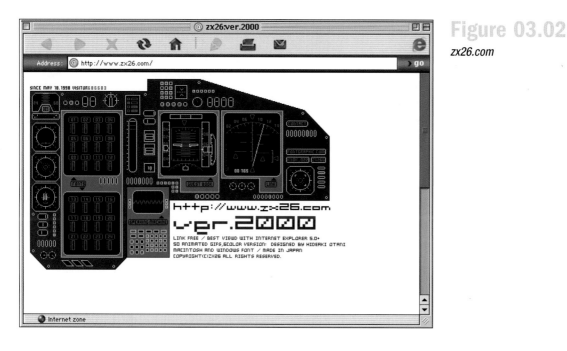

**Figure 03.02**

*zx26.com*

Midway through 2000, Cina left Desmond and Kral to pursue a solo design career, and some of his best work has been done since. Cina continues to refine the Grid-Based Icon Style at trueistrue, his experimental site. Many of his recent Flash animations contain over 100 Illustrator layers, each layer revealing itself in due time throughout the sometimes 30-minute long animation sequences. Such layering would lead to ugly clutter pretty quickly in a static gif or jpeg, but Flash allows for time-released design, where different elements build on each other to gradually form new and unexpected resonances. Cina's new work in Flash takes the Grid-Based Icon Style to its next logical level—from pop song to orchestral fugue.

Did I mention this style is good for making web sites too?

Cina is not the only web designer using chartjunk and grid-based Illustrator shapes as abstract design elements, but he is the one who popularized the style. Other web designers have chosen to incorporate the chartjunk gadgetry of retro-electronic interfaces into their web design (**Figure 03.02**). And at least one other designer regularly incorporates chartjunk from Photoshop itself.

The purpose of all this fake, stylized "interface" is to gently ridicule the hype of "web interactivity." In the beginning, the web was all futuristic and techno—chrome bevels, chunky knobs, and harsh drop shadows. Grid-based icon designers are well beyond that type of ugly pseudo-function, but they still pay homage to it in a mature, ironic way. The good news for commercial designers is that grid-based icon sites look clean, hip, "Scandinavian," and digital, while still avoiding the cartoonish excesses of the SuperTiny SimCity Style.

# Case Studies

Commercially, the Grid-Based Icon Style is applicable to almost any purpose. This chapter examines a Nike site for women, a snowboard enthusiast site for teens, and a news portal for the country of Serbia. That's quite a range of applications.

Because of its officious, techno-blueprint vibe, the Grid-Based Icon Style can be used to market cars, bikes, shoes, clothing, and anything else meant to seem "engineered." Because of its clean Bauhaus influence, the Grid-Based Icon Style can be used to lend an intelligent, hip look to just about anything else, from e-zines to pop bands to chocolate. And because of its playful, iconic side, this style is particularly appealing to teens. You know—kids, screenagers, the Playstation generation. (No, not you. You're a grown-up, remember?)

## Mike Cina: Mies Van Der Rohe Meets Kid A

An avid student of 20th century design and typography, Mike Cina didn't just pull the Grid-Based Icon Style out of thin air. Cina's grid-based layouts were inspired by Hofmann and Ruder. His use of color was inspired by Albers and Itten. But Cina's real genius was to synthesize the craft-centric aesthetics of these and other Bauhaus luminaries with the structured irony of post-modern bands such as Radiohead and DJ Spooky—all in the context of the web. To his peers in the underground web design community, Cina is known as a designer's designer, due in part to his proficiency in print and typography, his meticulous attention to detail, and his relentless experimentation.

Cina's style is somehow simultaneously intricate and minimalistic (**Figure 03.03**). Most immature designers are right up in your face with every single element they've concocted. It's as if they've worked so hard to create their groovy filter effects and their funky 3D shapes that they can't bear to let any part of their design take a backseat. Cina's design is much more ambient. Concise, strong elements take the foreground and define the form, while intricate background elements add resonance and richness to the overall layout. In this piece for *Wired* magazine, the foreground elements are solid and brightly colored shapes, while the background elements are thin, muted, diagrammatic lines. Note how the background lines are "in dialogue" with the foreground shapes. Numerous visual motifs are going on here, yet no one element is orphaned. This heightened sense of composition and balance is what sets Mike Cina apart from the wanna-bes.

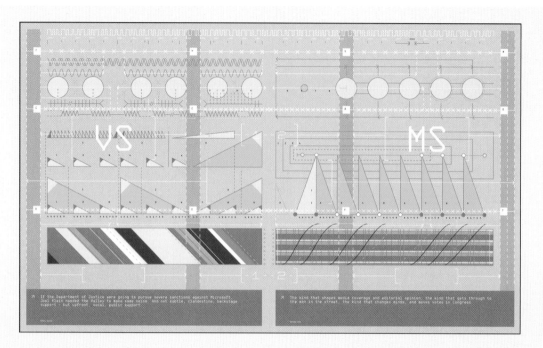

## Figure 03.03

*Wired Magazine comp*

Cina's designs are not always so intricate and austere. Much of his work is quite direct, and some pieces are even playful (**Figure 03.04**). This splash page is not "interactive" per se, but it is still built with the browser window in mind. You have to scroll to see the entire picture, and as you scroll down, the repeated window pattern creates a surprising op art/vertigo effect.

Cina's best web pieces thus far are his ambient Flash animations. Most Flash on the web falls into two categories. There is "splash Flash," built on the film narrative model: Images appear in a specified sequence, in rapid succession, synched to an audio track. There are usually flying letters and logos and shapes, all moving toward the end of the animation.

The other main type of Flash is "site Flash," entire sites made out of Flash, taking

advantage of Flash's "interactive" capabilities. Flash sites basically operate like normal (D)HTML sites, with some extra advantages (no wrestling with cross-browser/platform compatibility) and some extra disadvantages (they are difficult to bookmark and index).

Cina's Flash animations fall into neither category. They are much slower and less linear than most "splash Flash." Their slow pace is a reaction to the "click here quick" hyperactivity of blinking banner ads. With everything on the web battling and clamoring for user attention, Cina decided to take the opposite approach at **trueistrue.com**. A visit to trueistrue is like a calming breath of fresh air on an otherwise overheated web. Sometimes a visitor has to wait 5 or 10 minutes before he's even given the opportunity to click on anything. Other times, there's nothing to click on at all.

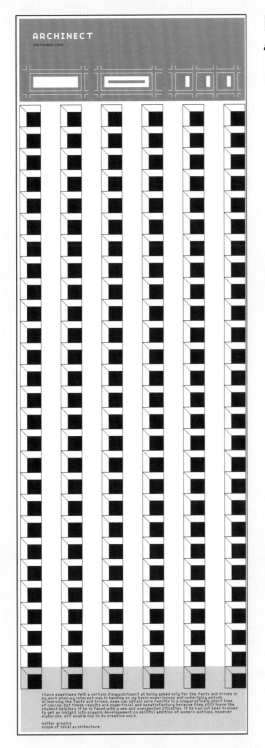

Figure 03.04
*archinect.com*

The genius of these Flash designs is that, as they grow and evolve, they still look great, regardless of what transitional state they are in. Here are three stills from the same Flash animation (**Figures 03.05** through **03.07**). Notice how each still is tightly designed in and of itself. In Flash, Cina can explore the relationship of design elements to each other not just in physical space, but in temporal "space" as well, over time. As these designs grow, recede, evolve, and dissipate, each element within the design remains in constant yet changing dialogue with every other element. Such "singing, dancing" design is simply not possible on a static printed page.

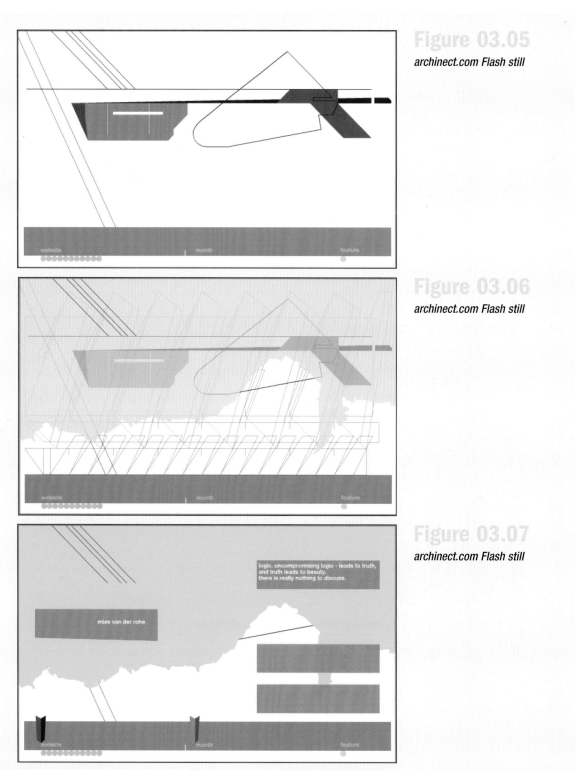

**Figure 03.05**

*archinect.com Flash still*

**Figure 03.06**

*archinect.com Flash still*

**Figure 03.07**

*archinect.com Flash still*

logic. uncompromising logic - leads to truth,
and truth leads to beauty.
there is really nothing to discuss.

mies van der rohe

# Nike Women: A Blueprint for Business

So far, I've discussed only personal, experimental work. But these same grid-based, geometric layouts work just as well in commercial settings. The Nike Women site (designed by Lars Cortsten and featuring a Mike Cina font), is a good commercial example of the Grid-Based Icon Style in action (**Figure 03.08**). Note the blueprint vibe and the intricately layered pseudo-functional detail work so common to this style.

Nike Women is a combination of Flash and HTML, but it's so seamless, you might not notice. All the lines in the lightly colored center strip to the right of the woman's figure are part of a Flash animation. Other than that strip, the rest of the page is comprised of static gif images. As the lines and shapes in the Flash animation move, they intersect and play off of the lines and angles in the static gifs, unifying the entire page so that it doesn't look like a static HTML "frame" surrounding a Flash animation "window" (even though that's technically what's happening).

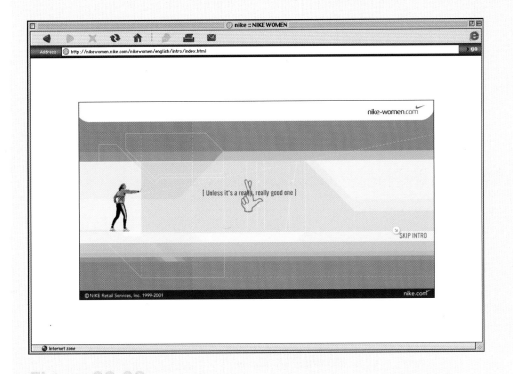

Figure 03.08

*nikewomen.nike.com/nikewomen*

## Figure 03.09

*nikewomen.nike.com/nikewomen*

Throughout the rest of the Nike Women site, the main HTML navigation menu resides at the top of each section, while Flash continues to handle the task of displaying the core content pieces (**Figure 03.09**). Note how the top navigation menu is curved at the edges so that the rest of the page flows up around it. This simple design technique goes a long way toward unifying an otherwise separate menu bar with the rest of the page.

At Nike Women, abstract areas of color and shape become elegant, non-boxy content areas, all pieced together at interesting 45-degree angles.

# Serbia: Aesthetic Usability

What if you don't want drastic geometric shapes, and what if you don't want a predominantly Flash site? The Grid-Based Icon Style still delivers, as Mike Cina's site for the country of Serbia clearly demonstrates (**Figure 03.10**). This site (which never did go live) was to be a news portal. Consequently, it had to be usable, text-centric, and easily navigable. And yet at the same time, the clients wanted something memorable and distinctive, not just another Netscape/Yahoo!/Altavista.

Cina adds distinction and flair by using cutout divots and dashed lines, cleverly side-stepping the standard boxy look currently plaguing most large content sites. The various bold colors not only look good, but they also serve to demarcate content areas. Cina even manages to include some signature icons in the top-left menu. With all the content on this page, you'd think it would be more cluttered, more bounded, more obviously partitioned. But Cina's aesthetic sense of composition here serves a less-abstract purpose—namely, to make this site easy and enjoyable to use. The Serbia site proves that quality graphic design always enhances usability, provided that the graphic designer knows what the heck he's doing.

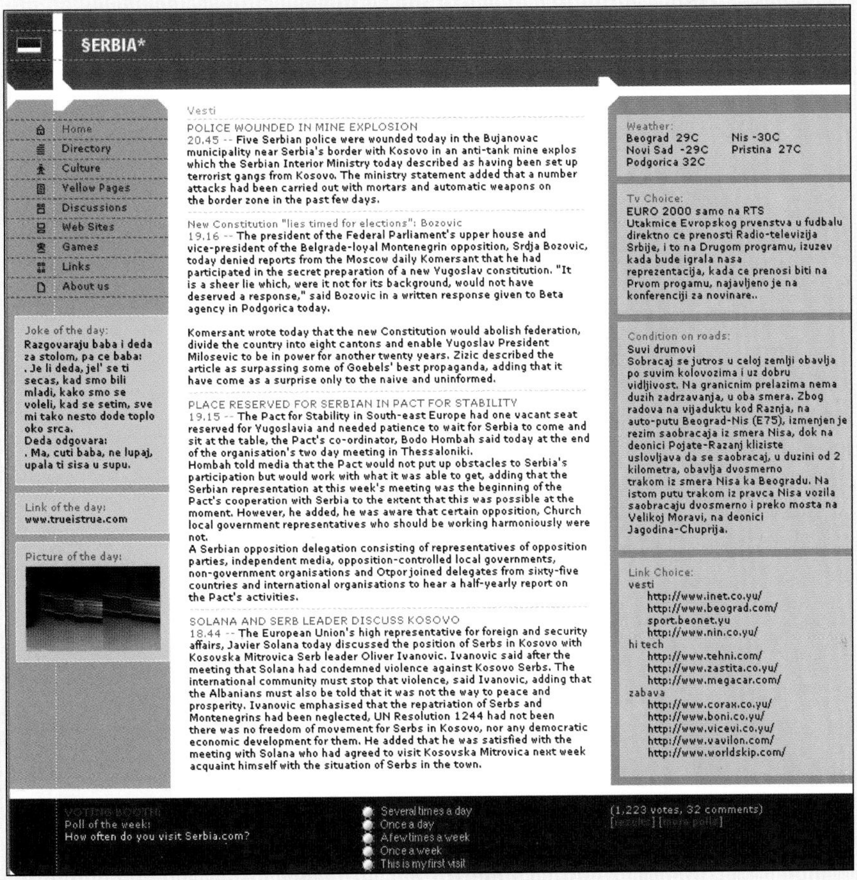

**Figure 03.10**

*Serbia comp*

# Techniques

Because grid-based icon design is based largely on intuition and experience. I've chosen to avoid a "connect-the-dots" approach, focusing instead on some basic principles and underlying methodologies. What really makes this style sing is a sense of balance and composition—although Illustrator plays its part as well.

## Creating Geometric Shapes at 45-Degree-Angle Increments

All geometric, grid-based layouts start with a grid. (Amazing, but true.) To establish your grid, first open a new document in Adobe Illustrator, and under **View**, first select **Show Grid**, and then select **Snap to Grid**. It's probably also a good idea to go to **File**, **Preferences**, **Guides & Grid...** and change your **Subdivisions** from **8** to **4**. It all depends on the level of detail you want to achieve, but if you have too many grid lines, your shapes snap to almost everything, rendering the "snap to grid" feature meaningless.

Next, begin creating the shapes and lines you want, and drag them where you want them in relation to each other on the grid. This, of course, is the creative part that I can't teach you. It helps to turn off the grid periodically (**View**, **Hide Grid**) to get a feel for what your design looks like without the grid—how it will ultimately appear. If by some happy accident you discover that certain grid lines are actually improving the balance of your layout between one shape and the next, you can always replicate those grid lines in your own design.

To achieve the classic Grid-Based Icon Style, it's best to stick to angles in increments of 45 degrees (45, 90, 135). Limiting yourself to these angles transfers that grid-based blueprint feel into your final design.

Be sure to save related design elements on the same layer and to use multiple layers. The value of such layering becomes apparent as you begin exporting these designs into other programs.

## Step 1: Save as Gifs

When you're satisfied with your design, it's time to prepare it for the web. To save your vectorized shapes as gifs, first take them through Photoshop. In Illustrator, choose **File**, **Export**. In the resulting dialog box, choose **Format**, **Photoshop 5**, and then click **Save**. When the Photoshop Options dialog box appears, be sure that **Anti-alias** and **Write Layers** are checked, and that under **Color Model**, **RGB** is selected. For **Resolution**, you might want to choose **Screen (72 dpi)**, but your Illustrator design will scale larger or smaller without any loss of quality, so just choose the size that makes the most sense for your web page. (The larger the dpi, the greater the dimensions of the image in pixels.)

Next, open your exported Illustrator file in Photoshop. Your layers should still be intact. Save your shapes as gifs, and call them into your web page as desired. Why start in Illustrator and then export to Photoshop? Why not just do the entire layout in Photoshop? Generally because Illustrator allows more control over vectorized shapes. But you could conceivably do the entire thing in Photoshop if you wanted to.

## Step 2: Save as Flash Animations

What if you want to create a Flash animation out of your original Illustrator design? This time, in Illustrator, go to **File**, **Save as**, and under **Format**, choose **Illustrator**. A dialog box appears, giving you several compatibility options. Make sure you choose a compatibility level that is supported by your particular version of Flash. For instance, Flash 4 on the Mac won't import Illustrator 8 files, so you'd better save your design as an Illustrator 7 file, or Flash won't be able to import it.

Next, open Flash, and choose **File**, **Import**. A dialog box appears. Locate and select your Illustrator file, and then click the **Import** button. This calls your original Illustrator design into Flash as vector art, preserving your original layers. Now it is up to you (and your killer Flash tutorial of choice) to set these shapes in motion. Sometimes Mike Cina sends his shapes down a fast and furious motion guide, but more often than not, he gradually fades each layer into view, either after a set amount of time or in response to a user mouse click. This is why it is so important to separate your design elements into meaningful layer groups back in Illustrator.

Why not just do the entire design in Flash? Again, because Illustrator allows more control over the creation of vector shapes than does Flash. Flash has enough to do without also having to double as line art creation software (which it does anyway).

# Melding Photography with Grid-Based Layouts

One of the most exciting aspects of the Grid-Based Icon Style is the way it incorporates photography into its grid-based, shape-centric layouts (**Figure 03.11**). Photographs aren't merely confined to tiny square frames within the shapes. Instead, a single photographic image occupies a large, unbounded space in the middle of the design, with the natural lines in the photograph serving as suggestive points of departure for the vector lines and shapes that follow.

In this print ad for Morphic ski gear, Cina uses the horizon line as a starting point for his layout. Notice how this design is an even balance between line art and photograph, with neither aspect dominating. This balanced "dialogue" between computer-generated art and real-world image gives this layout interest and tension. Just as the photograph leads to the creation of certain vector elements, it can work the other way too. Certain vector patterns can in turn lead to the manipulation of the original photograph. Notice how the skier's legs are transformed into abstract shapes.

These melded photo-vector designs are a great way to lend an air of techno-engineering to any real-world product. The only drawback is that they load slower than either a pure photographic jpeg or a pure line-art gif. The solution is to cut up your picture, saving the photo-intense elements as jpegs and the shape-intense elements as gifs. Where the two elements overlap, you'll just have to test both compression formats and see which works best. Note that jpeg compression is lossy and thus estimates the lines and colors of your shapes, sometimes rendering them incongruous with the lines and colors of their neighboring gif shapes. As always, it's a matter of splitting the difference between perfect rendering and quick downloading.

## Figure 03.11

*Morphic print ad*

# Using Chartjunk as Design

Grid-based icon designers love to take abstract chartjunk and incorporate it into web page design. At hoggorm, screenshots of rulers from the Photoshop program itself serve as the site's borders (**Figure 03.12**). Part of good "screen design" is being aware of the browser window. Regardless of how a page is built, it is almost always framed by a browser—a browser whose appearance has been largely predetermined by a software company. A designer can fight the tyranny of the browser frame with pop-up windows, "full-screening," and downloadable browser "skins," or he can make the best of it.

Hoggorm's designer, Marius Gronvold, makes the best of the browser frame by consciously alluding to it in his site design. For example, most designers wouldn't dare put a browser-generated slider in the middle of their page. But at hoggorm, this approach works, because the surrounding Photoshop rulers recontextualize the slider, making it fit into the page. Rather than ignoring the existence of browser chartjunk (as almost every other site does), hoggorm instead embraces browser chartjunk in order to repurpose it.

**Figure 03.12**

*anart.no/~hoggorm/*

The Grid-Based Icon Style has a plethora of web applications, from branding high-tech athletic shoes to clearly presenting Eastern European news. Grid-based icon designers have been criticized for their hard-core emphasis on historic graphic design techniques. "On the web," some would say, "we need to stick to the basics. All of this fancy-pants design just gets in the way."

Actually, nothing could be further from the truth. The students of the Bauhaus spent decades wrestling with composition and balance in order to make more functional objects. Exposure to and study of this rich arts and crafts heritage can only lead to better-crafted, more functional websites. The Grid-Based Icon Style proves that Bauhaus design isn't just for architecture and furniture anymore. Roll over, Walt Gropius, and tell Kandinsky the news.

# Sites Mentioned in This Chapter

http://www.testpilotcollective.com

http://www.trueistrue.com

http://www.mikecina.com

http://www.zx26.com

http://www.archinect.com

http://nikewomen.nike.com/nikewomen/

http://www.anart.no/~hoggorm/

"Come
Doused in mud
Soaked in bleach
As I want you to be
As a trend
As a friend
As an old memory."

—Nirvana

If there is indeed "nothing new under the sun" (as the author of *Ecclesiastes* repeatedly asserts), one way to come up with a "fresh" style is to go back in time a few decades, cut what you find, and paste it into the present. In the '60s and early '70s, digital printing was commercially unknown. The psychedelic Haight-Ashbury concert posters of Peter Max, the pop-art soup cans of Andy Warhol, and the loose pen-and-ink illustrations of Ralph Steadman were all created nondigitally and printed on offset presses. The more grassroots the art movement, the less precise the printing quality. This resulted in posters with color bleeding, smudges, and irregularities. In other words, a lot of low-fidelity printwork was floating around popular culture at the time.

Of course, in the '60s and early '70s, this nondigital print look was not "retro." It would not have even been considered "nondigital," because there was no digital printing with which to compare it. It was simply the way a lot of graphic design looked at the time.

Fast-forward to the early '90s. Iconoclastic graphic designer David Carson is turning heads everywhere with the unorthodox look of his new underground magazine, *Raygun*. Amidst a design culture hip-deep in the orderly, grid-based layouts that a new wave of desktop publishing software has made possible, Carson opts instead for a looser, dirtier, grungier style. His font sizes vary widely within the same layout. His line leading is intentionally off, causing his lines to blur into each other, overlapping and intersecting, the text itself becoming a kind of abstract art. Carson uses mostly distressed "grunge" fonts—fonts that bleed around the edges, fonts that aren't crisp and clean, fonts that look an awful lot like the predigital underground poster fonts of the late '60s. Imagine that.

In the early '90s, at a time when design is supposed to be "seen and not heard," serving the content it presents without drawing attention to itself, Carson forges a highly visible (some would say obtrusive) design style. His attitude and philosophy will have a major impact on the Lo-Fi Grunge Style of web design, so a brief exposure to some of his thoughts on graphic design seems appropriate here:

- **On the purpose of "hard to read" design:**

  "[In every issue of *Raygun*], there is almost always one [article] that's more difficult to read than some of the others, but... the starting point is not 'Well, let's muck this one up.' The starting point is to try to interpret the article, and doing that, some of them get harder to read, OK? I don't have a problem with that, and I really think it makes it more interesting to the reader, especially our reader, where you're competing with all these other things [like music video and computers]."

- **On the weakness of unobtrusive design:**

  "I believe now, if the type is invisible, so is your article, and it's probably not going to get read, because—at least with this audience, and I think it's spreading out more—they're seeing better TV, they're watching video screens. You give somebody a solid page of grey type and say, 'Read this brilliant story,' and a lot of people, they're going to go, 'Doesn't look very interesting. Let's try and find something more interesting.' I think if it's invisible, it's just done a horrible disservice to what's potentially a really good article."

Fast-forward yet again, this time to the latter half of the '90s. Location: Helsinki, Finland. Teenage design savant Miika Saksi is devouring issues of *Elle* and other fashion magazines, studying, absorbing, learning Photoshop, tweaking, experimenting, honing his style. Although Carson is not Saksi's strongest direct influence, the international fashion magazines that Saksi is reading are laid out by designers who are only too conversant with Carson's work.

When Saksi finally takes his work to the web in 1997, he dramatically impacts the underground online design community. Up to this point, design on the web has been largely grid-based, boxy, controlled, digital, and clean. Saksi manages to combine the irregular printing idiosyncrasies of the late '60s with Carson's loose, antigrid layouts—webifying both without losing any of their analog charm, and adding a dash of his own Euro-fashion design influence to the mix for good measure. The Lo-Fi Grunge Style of web design is born.

# As Close to Print as the Web Should Get

Most of the "craft" of lo-fi grunge design is accomplished in Photoshop—experimenting with brushes, compounding layers, applying filters to selected images, and overtly incorporating some form of distressed text into the overall collage. This Photoshop "design" is then sliced into parts, saved as gifs or jpegs, and pieced back together into a web page. So I'm not offering these sites as examples of information architecture or even sensible navigation.

Because so much of lo-fi grunge relies on Photoshop rather than HTML for its distinctiveness, it runs the risk of being labeled print-centric. Indeed, many of these design collages would be better represented at 300 dpi, gracing the pages of some glossy print magazine. So if the point of this book is to break away from mere repurposed print design, why am I offering up lo-fi grunge as a fresh web design style? Primarily because on the web, where everything is so clean and partitioned, lo-fi grunge does stand out as fresh. And because it is derived from a nonstandard, dirty, experimental print style, I'm willing to overlook its print origins and admit it as a web-specific design style.

Rather than spend a lot of time talking about Photoshop techniques (there are already a few books on the subject), I explain some of the fundamental design and coding hacks that make lo-fi grunge "work" on the web, taking advantage of the web's unique strengths and working around some of its nonprint peculiarities. But before tackling the techniques, check out some of the following lo-fi grunge sites.

# Case Studies

Initially, lo-fi grunge was used to make slick online magazines about fashion, skateboarding, snowboarding, fashion, and fashion. These e-zines were really just excuses for design showcasing (as evidenced by the fact that several "issues" of Saksi's *Silbato* e-zine have no content whatsoever). The Lo-Fi Grunge Style has since been used to make a very navigable site for a bicycle tire company and a groovy snowboard retail site. Lo-fi grunge's commercial applications are broader than teen recreation and fashion, but those are its initial points of departure. Any product marketed to the "extreme sports" sector is ripe for lo-fi grunge design. This includes all-terrain automobiles, cross-training athletic shoes, sports drinks, soft drinks, jet skis, and Taco Bell.

# Saksi's Personal Sites: Faux-Functional Finnish Fashion Fodder

Miika Saksi maintains a cryptic labyrinth of interlinked URLs. *Smallprint* is his online fashion/culture magazine with little content but lots of different covers and "coming soon" pages. *Silbato* is an online fashion/culture magazine, and *Sueellen* is an offline fashion/culture magazine that has an online presence. After its seventh issue, *Silbato* was subsumed into *Sueellen*—the eighth issue of *Silbato* became the first online issue of *Sueellen*. Simple, isn't it? Except for the fact that, once again, only one issue of *Silbato* actually has any content. The rest of its issues are just excuses for design. As such, surfing this nexus of sites can be very disorienting, especially if you don't speak Finnish. So I'm not offering these sites as examples of information architecture or even sensible navigation. Simply consider how they look.

One noticeable feature of Saksi's sites is that his pages don't resize to fill the browser window. Instead, his layouts are frozen, often starting in the top-left of the browser window and flowing downward to the right until they dissipate gradually into negative space (**Figure 04.01**). Although this type of layout ignores certain strengths of the web as a design medium, it still manages to look "unscrunched." If you visit **smallprint.net** with your browser window at 1000 pixels wide, the layout is still unobjectionable, despite the fact that it occupies only 640 pixels of horizontal window space. How is this accomplished?

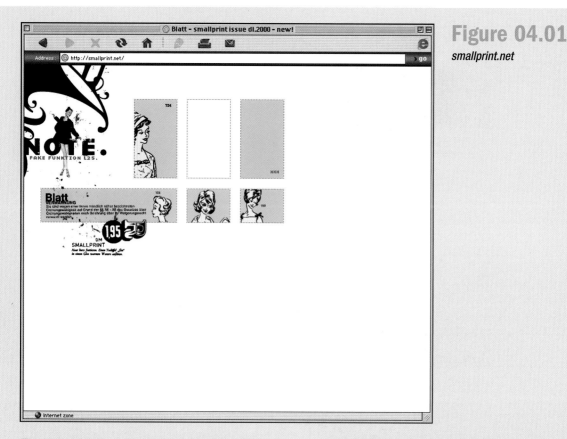

Figure 04.01

*smallprint.net*

First, the design elements in the top-left corner seem to originate somewhere outside of the browser window itself. This is Saksi's way of saying, "I know I'm cramped up in the corner here. I did it on purpose." His loose design spills down into the page, finally taking a more structured form in the green boxes. There is no learnable formula for this particular design solution. The point is that Saksi is intentionally designing for a browser window, not for a printed page.

This layout doesn't look bad in a large window because its background is white, and there is no strong demarcating right border to tell you where the 640 pixel-wide design ends. As such, the negative space below and to the right of the collage is "invited" to become part of the intentional design.

Another way Saksi manages to make negative space seem like part of his collage is by using Photoshop brushes. Brushes are simply patterns that irregularly filter what would otherwise be straightforward lines or marks. Brushes create that smudgy, inconsistent, analog printing press look. By making brush marks at the edge of his collage and causing them to seemingly bleed over into the negative space, Saksi forms a continuity between his image and the negative space.

At other times, Saksi overcomes the unknown dimensions of the browser window by intentionally limiting his design to very small areas (**Figure 04.02**). It's as if he's saying, "I give up trying to fill this whole screen, because I can't figure out how big it is. I'm just going to make this one part of the

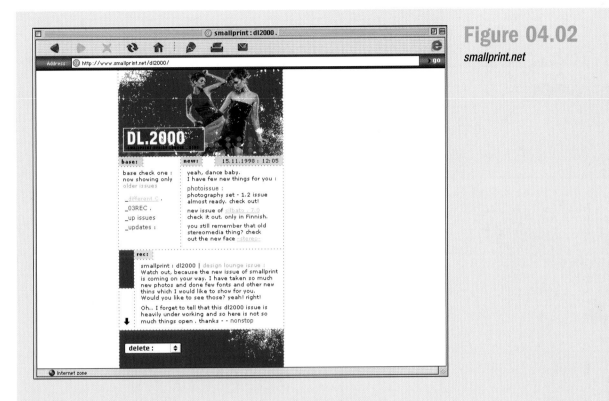

**Figure 04.02**

*smallprint.net*

screen look really good in and of itself and then cause you to focus on it."

Although there have been new liquid layout design advancements since the heyday of lo-fi grunge in 1998, Saksi's narrow strips of information still have a refreshing, relaxing visual quality. Most people these days try to jam-pack their pages with as much information as possible. In contrast, a site that has only a thin column of design and text doesn't overloaded its visitor with input. Consequently, said visitor can focus his undepleted attentions all the more intently on the strip of information he is given. One objection to these thin strips of information is that they force the visitor to scroll more. And the spirit of David Carson would say,

"Wonderful. A bit of intentional scrolling challenges the visitor and gets him involved."

You've noted the smudges. You've noted the misaligned grunge fonts. You've noted the frozen screen layouts. You've noted the TV-esque scanlines. What? You say you haven't noted the TV-esque scanlines? OK. Note the TV-esque scanlines (**Figure 04.03**). These scanlines, like the smudges, are meant to give the web page a more analog look. Whereas the smudges simulate "analog" printing, the scanlines simulate analog television, subtly acknowledging the fact that web surfers are actually looking at a screen. I talk more about scanlines and brushes in the "Techniques" section.

**Figure 04.03**
*smallprint.net*

Finally, let's not overlook the use of fashion models as design elements. If you're designing a site that doesn't exactly warrant the blatant parading of fashion models across the page (and yes, there are those rare instances when fashion models simply won't do), any human body will suffice. Just make sure the body you use is free-floating on the background of your design, with its outlines visible. A torso inside a square photograph won't have the same effect, because it won't be reckoned in the context of the overall design.

An interesting result of this designerly use of human bodies (models or otherwise) has to do with scale. By interjecting human figures into your design, you can make your other design elements seem huge or miniscule by comparison (**Figure 04.04**). Since everyone naturally identifies with the scale of their own bodies, using human bodies as design elements is a way to interject an objective scalar benchmark into your work, allowing you to then tweak and manipulate that baseline proportional scale to suit your own reality-distorting purposes.

Figure 04.04

*factory512.com*

## Grungy Commerce:
## Nokian Tyres

Lest you're thinking there could be no commercial application whatsoever for lo-fi grunge, consider the Nokian Tyres site (**Figure 04.05**), again designed by Saksi. There are still the narrow columns, the scanlines, and the brushes, but here Saksi abandons the gridless layout for a more partitioned look. Note that his border of choice is simply tiny dashes (on other sites he uses tiny dots). Dashes work surprisingly well as borders in web pages, especially considering their ease of implementation.

Saksi uses a solid-color block at the top of the page and then repeats that color in the nav bar to indicate hierarchical location, as

any good usability expert would suggest. The site is clean, navigable, and readable, yet still "cutting-edge" enough to appeal to your average quasi-daring, thirty-something mountain biker.

The Nokian Tyres site is a perfect example of how such a seemingly design-centric style can be employed to serve a commercial purpose. Miika even sneaks in a grungy typewriter font to list the tire specifications. The typewriter font works well in this context, because the entire web page is set up to resemble a printed product specification sheet that a reseller might receive from a manufacturer.

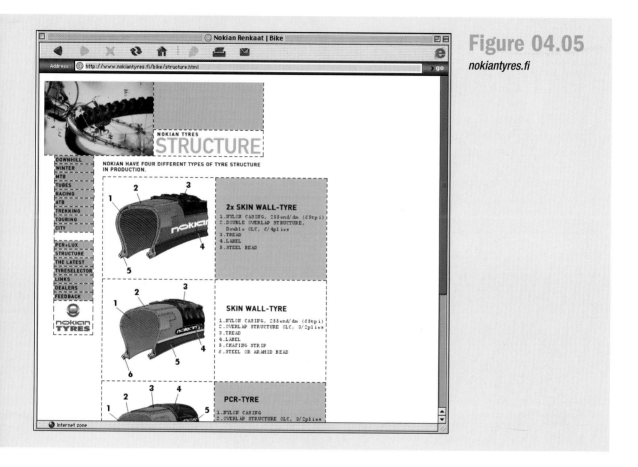

**Figure 04.05**

*nokiantyres.fi*

# Techniques

The lion's share of lo-fi grunge design work is done in Photoshop, but it still pays to keep the peculiarities of the web in mind. Lo-fi grunge sites are not just huge Photoshop collages saved as jpegs and called into an HTML page. Some pre-web planning and manipulation are required.

# Background/Foreground Gif Pairing

Although most lo-fi grunge layouts don't resize, there is a way to fill the entire screen by cleverly pairing foreground transparent gifs with tiling background gifs (**Figure 04.06**). How can Saksi make the horizontal stripe fill the entire browser window without knowing how large the window is? He could simply make the foreground image huge (1800×1200) so that it would safely fill most monitors. But an 1800×1200-pixel image takes a long time to load, even if 75 percent of it is only solid areas of color.

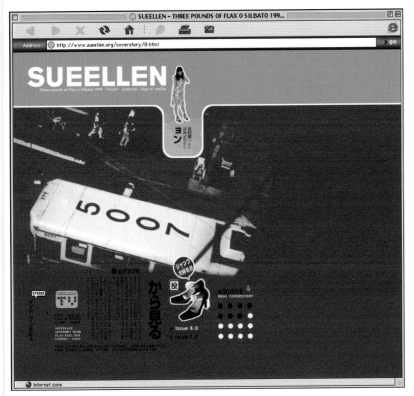

Figure 04.06

*sueellen.org*

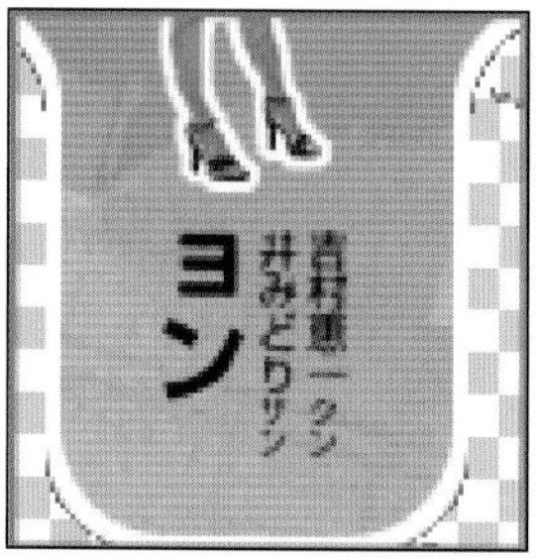

## Figure 04.07

*Foreground gif (the checkered area is transparent)*

Here is a foreground gif from the previous Sueellen page (**Figure 04.07**), and here is the page's tiling background gif (**Figure 04.08**). None of the page's foreground images extend beyond 600 pixels wide. Only the tiling background continues sideways. But because the background stripe is incorporated into the foreground design, it seems like one seamless, full-screen picture.

This technique is relatively simple to implement:

1. Design your layout in Photoshop, making sure to include a repeating horizontal element that you'd like to extend to the end of the browser window.

2. Isolate that repeating "stripe" element as a separate image. This will be your background image. Make it at least 20 pixels wide and 1500 pixels high so that your horizontal "stripe" doesn't unceremoniously reappear at the bottom of someone's gigantic monitor. Save this 20×1500-pixel image, and call it into your HTML via <body background="yourimage.gif">.

3. Save the rest of your foreground design, slicing it into chunks so that it loads faster. Save as transparent gifs any chunks of your foreground design that need to let the background show through.

4. Position these foreground design chunks over your tiling background (preferably using CSS layer position-ing, although here Saksi uses tables).

## Figure 04.08

*Tiling background gif*

That's it. You now have what appears to be a huge full-screen image, without the technical drawbacks of actually having a huge full-screen image.

This same tiling background hack can also be used to make vertically tiling stripes. Follow the same steps, except this time use a vertical stripe in your design, and then make your background gif 1800 pixels wide and at least 20 pixels high. Now your background image tiles down instead of sideways, causing full-screen vertical stripes.

Pairing foreground elements with tiling background elements is just one more way to get the browser to work for you instead of your always working against it, trying in vain to make it act like a printed page.

# Scanlines

There are several ways to achieve the TV scanline effect. The most straightforward way is to alternate two lines, each 1 pixel high, of similar but slightly varying color values (for example, ff6666 and ff3333). Then just place this alternating two-line pattern in the background of your design as desired. To fill a large area with a small repeating pattern, first select the pattern you want to use and choose **Edit**, **Define Pattern**. Next, select the area you want to fill, and choose **Edit**, **Fill**. In the dialog box that appears, choose **Pattern** from the pull-down menu and click **OK**.

Another technique is to create your scanline pattern using the method just described, save it to its own Photoshop layer, and then place that scanline layer above the other layers in your collage that you want to affect. Next, simply decrease the opacity of the scanline layer until grooviness occurs. Flatten your Photoshop image, slice it into manageable pieces, and save those pieces as gifs or jpegs to be called into your web page.

A third, more drastic technique (for Mac users only) is to use Deep Devices' "RetroScan" Photoshop filter (freely downloadable from **http://shareware.cnet.com/shareware/1,10269,0-16170-501-0-1-3,00.html?qt=retroscan&ca=16170**). According to its creators, "RetroScan is a professional quality Photoshop Plug-In that simulates the effect of rescanning a noisy TV signal. It provides an easy way to achieve the fashionable 'cyber punk' effect for print, multimedia, and video." I couldn't have said it better myself. It really is a groovy piece of software, allowing you to customize scanline size, scanline intensity, image ghosting, and even the amount of TV "snow." Use it sparingly. A little goes a long way.

# Brushes for Smudges

Custom brushes are essential for achieving that smudged, misprinted look. You can download some nice premade brushes from **http://www.surfstation.lu/ 13.html**. To load these new brushes into your Photoshop brushes palette, go to your brushes window (choose **Window, Show Brushes**) and click on the arrow in the top-right corner of the window. From the options menu that appears, select **Load Brushes**. Then simply locate your newly downloaded brushes file and click on it. Your new brush patterns appear at the bottom of your brushes palette. (You might need to scroll down to find them.)

To create your own custom brushes, start with a 30×30-pixel document. Next, create a pattern in that document. You can use noise filters, draw lines yourself, or use any combination thereof. Once you get a pattern you think you like (you won't really know until you use it), open your brushes window and click on the arrow in the top-right corner. From the options menu that appears, choose **Define Brush**. Your newly created brush pattern now appears at the bottom of your brushes palette. Experiment with creating brushes until you get some that you like.

After you've selected the desired brush from your brushes palette by clicking on it, it's time to paint. Click on the pencil tool, and select a foreground color. For lo-fi grunge purposes, merely dab the brush; don't actually paint with it. You're trying to create a corrosive effect, not draw a line. You can create either an ink smudge or a misprint.

To create an ink smudge, match your pencil color to the color of the text you want to smudge. Next, create a new layer for your smudges, making sure your smudge layer is above your text layer. Next, click your pencil near the edges of your text. This might take some trial and error, but when you do it correctly, it appears as if a printing press has smeared some extra ink while printing your text. This is one way to begin "eroding" the sterile digitality of computer-based design.

To create a misprint effect, match your pencil color to the background color of your page. Next, create a layer for your misprint effects, and place your misprint layer above the other layers of your design that you want to effect. Then, click your pencil on an area that you want to seem misprinted. It should look as if the page's background is showing through your design, as if the "printing" in that particular area got worn off or didn't quite take.

These brush techniques are subtle, and they might not seem to make much difference. But God is in the details. Your visitors won't notice exactly what you've done, but they will notice that your site looks different—less digital and more physical.

# Motion Within a Collage

Finally, to bring these "print" collages to life on the web, incorporate an animated gif into the layout of your collage. Don't add an animated gif out to the side of your collage. Instead, pick an element that's already in your collage, and then animate it.

First, design your layout to include an element that would look good animated. At **mesoa.com**, for example, they chose to animate the screen of a television set (**Figure 04.09**). The television set is collaged in Photoshop along with the rest of the layout.

After you complete the collage, select the area you want to animate. In this case, the area is not the entire television, but just the screen. Animate that square area in a gif animation program, using whatever series of frames you like, and then save it as a gif. Next, cut up your original collage into squares, saving each square as a gif or jpeg.

There are two ways to call this collage into your web page. The old-school way is to use tables. This gets tricky, because your tiny animation square has to fit in with the rest of the collage, so you have to mind your splicing to make sure it does. A better solution is to use CSS layers. Put the entire collage, including the unanimated TV screen section, on one layer. Then put the animated gif on a top layer, positioning it absolutely so that it fits properly in the overall design.

The final effect brings an otherwise static image to life. Again, use this sparingly. The degree to which your visitor's attention is drawn to the animation is also the degree to which his attention is drawn away from the rest of the page.

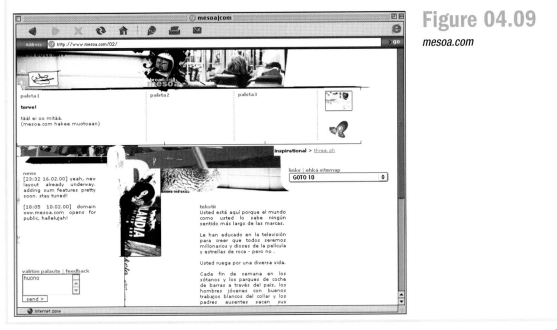

**Figure 04.09**

*mesoa.com*

The Lo-Fi Grunge Style of web design requires guesswork, experimentation, and a willingness to spend some time in Photoshop. Lo-fi grunge sites might seem loose and fun, but they are by no means haphazardly created. Knowing about brushes, scanlines, and tiling backgrounds can start you on your way to lo-fi grunge greatness. And if you're already skilled at this type of Carsonesque distressed print work, taking your talent to the web is simply a matter of course.

# Sites Mentioned in This Chapter

http://www.smallprint.net

http://www.sueellen.org

http://www.factory512.com

http://www.nokiantyres.fi

http://shareware.cnet.com/ shareware/1,10269,0-16170-501- 0-1-3,00.html?qt=retroscan&ca =16170

http://www.surfstation.lu/13.html

http://www.mesoa.com

"When I was their age I could draw like Raphael, but it took me a lifetime to learn to draw like them."

—Pablo Picasso
(after viewing a collection
of children's drawings)

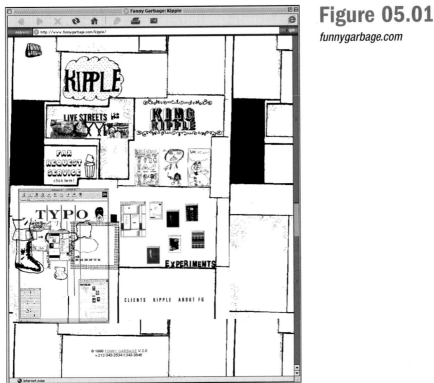

**Figure 05.01**

*funnygarbage.com*

This book is subtitled *Eye Candy from the Underground,* which means that the designers featured in this book are supposed to be from the underground. So how can I feature a design firm like Funny Garbage, whose clients include Warner Music Group, VH1, Cartoon Network, Comedy Central, Barnes & Noble, NASCAR, and Lego? I can feature them because their experimental site, Kipple (**Figure 05.01**), is as strange and creative a piece of web experimentation as you're likely to find. Due largely to Kipple, Funny Garbage gets credit for pioneering the Paper Bag Style of web design.

Ironically, the other main paper bag design firm discussed in this chapter, P2, has done work for Warner Music Group, VH1, MTV, Nickelodeon, The Sundance Channel, Toyota, and CDnow. Why is it that such a cartoonish, playful, seemingly sloppy design style is sported by two award-winning firms, both doing major work for major clients? Funny Garbage and P2 have a combined portfolio for which most design firms would sell their mothers. So why are their personal sites so misaligned, crinkly, and flawed?

One explanation is, "When you've got it, you don't have to flaunt it." Funny Garbage and P2 don't have to be trendy or flashy or futuristic or retro. Their commercial work speaks for itself. They've earned the right to relax, be expressive, and let it all hang out. In other words, they've earned the right to play. That being the case, why choose to play with asymmetrical fonts, scanned sketchbook drawings, and a mostly colorless palette?

Both firms seem to be expressing a sort of willful anarchy, a reaction against the professional elitism that frequently infects

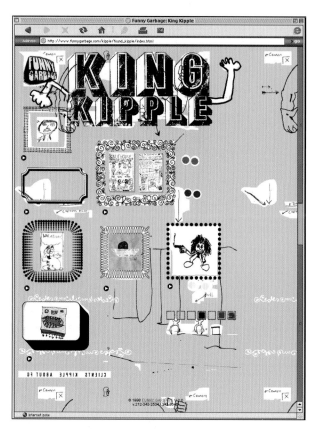

**Figure 05.02**

*funnygarbage.com*

the commercial design community. David Carson reacted against such design elitism with defiance and grunge. But when Carson's grunge style became fashionable, he was more than happy to inherit the mantle of the new design elite. Funny Garbage and P2 are reacting in a more self-depreciating, Dada way.

Ultimately, the adoption of this loose, "antidesign" style is simply a matter of personal preference. The founders of Funny Garbage have their roots in graffiti writing, and P2 is a design firm comprised entirely of two brothers. Make of these facts what you will, but both firms do enjoy their playing. I don't mean they enjoy experimenting with new graphical modes of expression. I mean they enjoy playing, like kids with finger

paints and crayons and glue and stuff. This is not a criticism. Based on the Picasso quotation at the beginning of this chapter, it is actually high praise.

Visually, the Paper Bag Style is even sloppier and more messed up than the Lo-Fi Grunge Style, while still avoiding the nightmarish and user-unfriendly excesses of the Pixelated Punk Rock Style. If the Lo-Fi Grunge Style hearkens back to the print look of 1969, the Paper Bag Style hearkens back to the print look of 1892. The former is retro; the latter is downright archival. The Paper Bag Style abounds with stylized arrows, ornate brackets, funky woodblock fonts, and all sorts of other extraneous frills and filigree (**Figure 05.02**). And, of course, there's the ubiquitous paper bag texture.

# Case Studies

Because of its whimsy, the Paper Bag Style is a logical fit for any sort of children's site, from the Cartoon Network to Nickelodeon to Etoys. At its most extreme, the Paper Bag Style can look like a hastily prepared, left-wing political pamphlet, useful for branding "vintage" blue jeans (as you can see on the Levi's Vintage site). I also examine two community sites where the Paper Bag Style has been applied more sparingly, adding personality and breaking monotony without hindering usability.

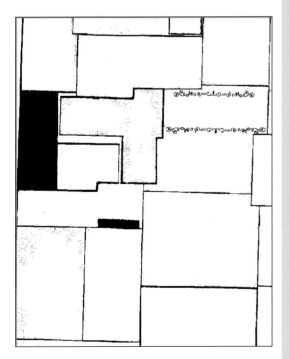

## Figure 05.03

*Tiling background gif*

# Funny Garbage's Kipple: MacGyver Does Web Art

On the classic and now defunct TV series *MacGyver,* the show's star was always kludging together some contraption from duct tape, Saran Wrap, and pipe cleaners that would catapult him over a 50-foot wall or allow him to pass safely through a field of land mines or some other such nonsense. If MacGyver ever built a web site, it would be Kipple, Funny Garbage's online experimental playground. Armed with just paper, pencils, a scanner, and gif animation technology, the Jedi at Funny Garbage manage to create a web site that's simultaneously engaging, hilarious, and groundbreaking.

One of Kipple's signature characteristics is massive full-screen clutter (**Figure 05.01**). Scrawled lines, goofy drawings, and paper crinkles are everywhere. The key to this effect is a large tiling background (in this case, 600×750 pixels) that leaves ample space for foreground images (**Figure 05.03**).

Why not just save the foreground and back-ground images together and call them in as a single image? Two reasons. First, with the foreground and background images separated, this funky abstract background can keep tiling to the right while the essential foreground images remain in focus on the left. Second, this background image is a greyscale, 16-color gif. Despite its large geographical size, it weighs only 9.2K. Saving the colorful foreground images as part of the background image would increase its file size dramatically.

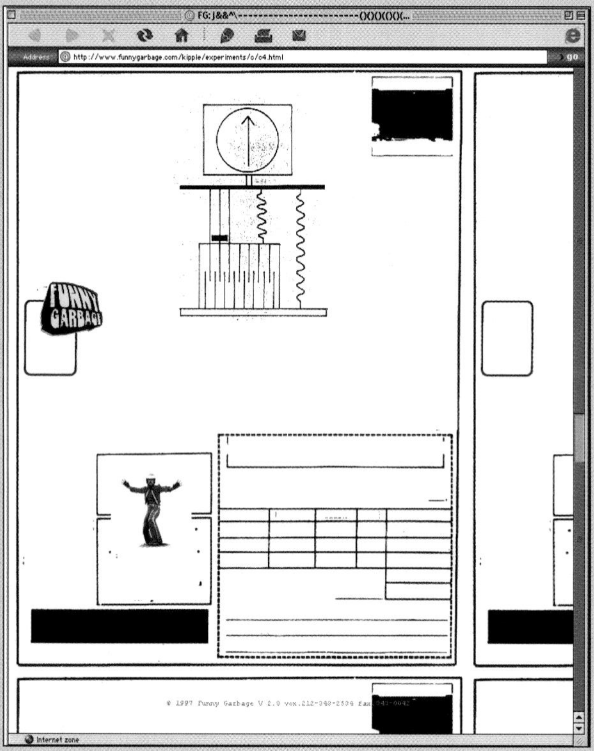

**Figure 05.04**

*funnygarbage.com*

Because this background image purposefully leaves space for the foreground images, the entire page takes on a collage effect—and a very irregular one at that. Yes, there are partitions and boundaries, but they are refreshingly crooked and asymmetrical. The trick is to comp the entire page in Photoshop first and then save the foreground and background elements separately. (I'll talk more about this in the "Techniques" section, under "Intentional Misalignment and Sloppy Boundaries.")

This tiling background is so large and irregularly patterned that, as it begins to repeat itself to the right, it still appears to be part of a single screen-sized image.

There is no "tiling" effect, because the background is broken up by foreground images on the left side, so your mind is unable to distinguish the "repeat."

Even when Kipple's page design is sparse and uncluttered (**Figure 05.04**), these large, irregular tiling backgrounds keep things active and "undigital." This particular page consists of one greyscale background gif, one foreground logo gif, and two foreground animated gifs (the guy waves his arms, and the machine springs up and down). The background is nothing more than some sort of lo-res, scanned-in, postal form. And yet the overall effect is striking, very unweblike, and gleefully brilliant.

**Figure 05.05**
*funnygarbage.com*

One of the advantages of purposefully going for a sloppier look is that you can get away with design *faux pas* that would otherwise look bad or wrong in a tidier context. For instance, at Kipple's "Live Streets," a photo gallery of graffiti and old vans, the featured images themselves are called in as tiling backgrounds (**Figure 05.05**).

Usually, a nonseamless tiling background like this looks amateurish, but with the navigation arrows in the foreground right on

top of the featured images, Funny Garbage is saying, "We know the background seams are showing. That's all part of our plan." This sloppy tiling background technique is perfect for the subject matter—bombed-out walls and rundown vehicles. And what an elegant navigational solution. Instead of partitioning off some distracting side bar or top bar to house their navigational elements, Funny Garbage simply puts their arrows right on top of the content itself. The navigation becomes part of the art.

# P2: The Kids Grow Up

Christopher and Matthew Pacetti have made a name for themselves in the design community by thinking way out of the box. Both have a background in fine arts, and they bring their painting and artistic influences to bear on their portfolio site, P2 (**Figure 05.06**). The core frame of the site is built in Flash around a billboard metaphor with five options. Click any of the options, and an animation transitions you to that section. Each section looks different, but always with the billboard metaphor present (**Figures 05.07** and **05.08**).

The metaphor is compelling and visually interesting precisely because it is off-center. Note the angular black lines in the background swooshing in from the top left. Note the diagonal line pointing to the "logo" in the top right. Like Kipple, rather than relegating the navigation elements to a sidebar, the navigation elements are built into the overall pictographic metaphor.

## Figure 05.06

*p2output.com*

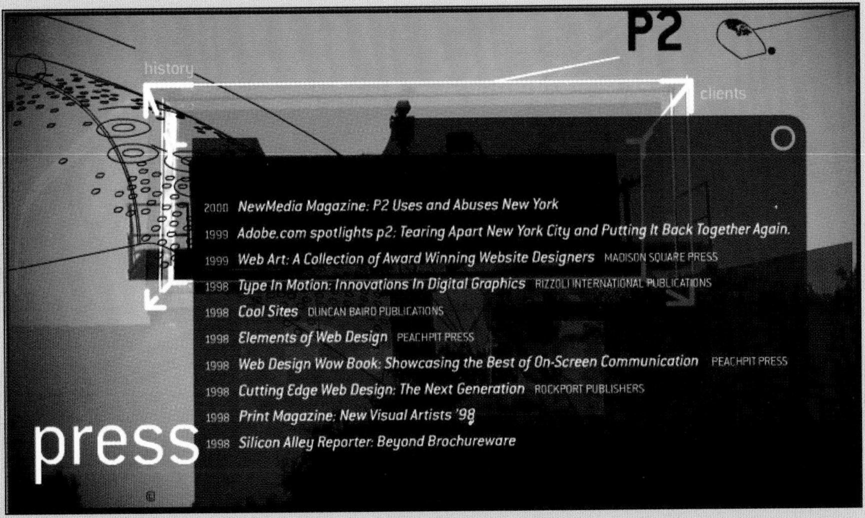
P2
history
clients
2000 NewMedia Magazine: P2 Uses and Abuses New York
1999 Adobe.com spotlights p2: Tearing Apart New York City and Putting It Back Together Again.
1999 Web Art: A Collection of Award Winning Website Designers MADISON SQUARE PRESS
1998 Type In Motion: Innovations In Digital Graphics RIZZOLI INTERNATIONAL PUBLICATIONS
1998 Cool Sites DUNCAN BAIRD PUBLICATIONS
1998 Elements of Web Design PEACHPIT PRESS
1998 Web Design Wow Book: Showcasing the Best of On-Screen Communication PEACHPIT PRESS
1998 Cutting Edge Web Design: The Next Generation ROCKPORT PUBLISHERS
1998 Print Magazine: New Visual Artists '98
1998 Silicon Alley Reporter: Beyond Brochureware
press

**Figure 05.07**

*p2output.com*

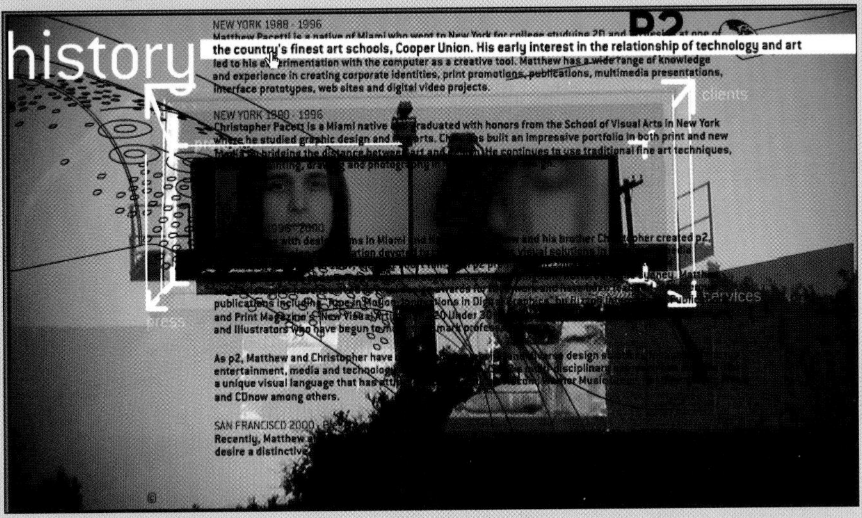
history
NEW YORK 1988 - 1996
the country's finest art schools, Cooper Union. His early interest in the relationship of technology and art
and experience in creating corporate identities, print promotions, publications, multimedia presentations,
interface prototypes, web sites and digital video projects.
clients
services
press

**Figure 05.08**

*p2output.com*

This busy background approach is all well and good, but what happens when it comes time to display some text on top? P2 solves this problem in two ways. When there's not a lot of text to be displayed, they simply shade the background a bit under the text, making it easier to read without wrecking the layout's overall aesthetics (**Figure 05.07**). When there is a lot of text to be displayed, P2 uses a rollover effect in Flash so that the line your cursor is on gets its own neutral, readable background, while the rest of the text remains unhighlighted (**Figure 05.08**). As you move your cursor down the page, the lines of text advance and recede according to your focus. Is this the best design approach for a multipage Perl scripting tutorial? No. But for a design firm portfolio site trying to present itself as creative, it's perfect—engaging without being too obtrusive.

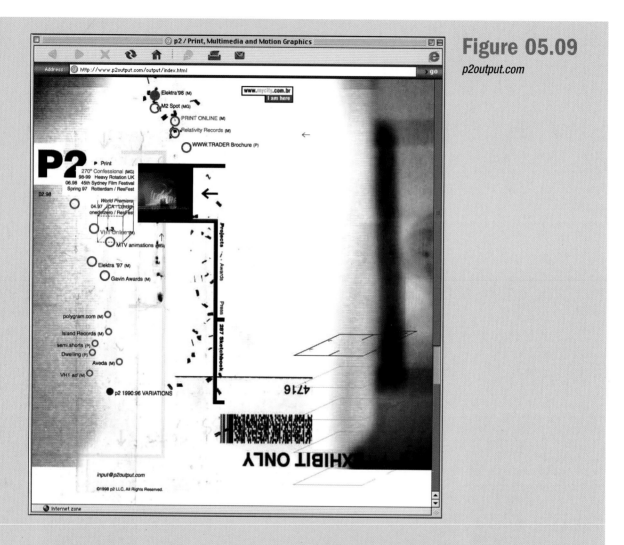

**Figure 05.09**

*p2output.com*

The paper bag ethic is also apparent in this early version of P2's core page (**Figure 05.09**). Note the misalignment and the large tiling background image. Rather than seeming comic and cartoonish like Kipple, this P2 page has a more mature, even futuristic, feel to it, due largely to the diagrammatic shapes, the blurry photographic background pattern, and the somber sans-serif type. P2 proves that you can be playful and still come across as mature. Actually, I think they call that particular combination of attributes "creative."

# Levi's Vintage: The Revolution Will Be Marketed

The perfect commercial example of extreme paper bagism is Levi's Vintage (**Figure 05.10**). The far-left navbar slides up and down, depending on the location of your cursor, and the second-level navbar to its right blurs in and out. Atop the entire body text, an animated line drawing proceeds at regular intervals, and to the far right, a QuickTime movie plays. That's four frames of animation all happening simultaneously and out of synch. Once you drill down to the actual clothing, things stop moving and calm down a bit. But the skewed parallelogram frames and asymmetrical fonts remain throughout.

This site is ripe for "usability criticism," most of which would be unfounded. The navigational hierarchy is actually very logical and followable. More to the point, this is not an e-commerce site. You can't buy clothes online here. This site is meant to brand a particular line of vintage clothing. In each section, a historical vibe is set, a brief story is told, and the clothes appropriate to that era are cataloged. If all goes well and the branding succeeds, I now associate the Levi's Striped Blazer with John and Yoko's "love-in." All that's left for me to do now is click on the "store finder" and then haul my nostalgic, peace-loving torso down to the nearest Levi's retailer. Mission accomplished.

When what you're selling is the myth of a bygone era, an era meant to be perceived as "faded and worn," to use a crisp, perfectly aligned futuristic design style is to shoot yourself in the foot. The Paper Bag Style is perfect for just this sort of "through a glass darkly" branding spiel.

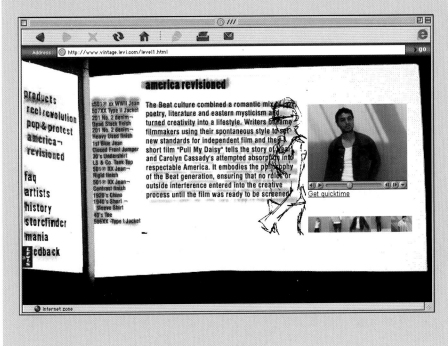

**Figure 05.10**

*vintage.levi.com*

# gURL and Ka-Ching:
# 25% Paper Bag Communities

If you don't feel brave enough to dump the Paper Bag Style full-force on your unsuspecting clients just yet, don't worry. You can still implement this style to a lesser degree. gURL (**Figure 05.11**) and Ka-Ching (**Figure 05.12**) are two community sites that both benefit from a restrained use of paper bagism. gURL is visibly more torn and skewed than Ka-Ching, but the former is for teen girls, and the latter is for career women. On Ka-Ching, the paper bag influence really only appears in the torn tabs at the top and in the section header type.

Note that both sites are quite readable and partitioned. In both instances, the Paper Bag Style adds charm and lightheartedness without hindering usability. These subtle design touches encourage visitors to "own" a community site. It becomes their site, bookmarked and visited regularly—not just because they identify with the content, but because the site sports their style. When designing a targeted community site, using a "safe" copycat style actually risks invalidating your site's credibility with its target audience.

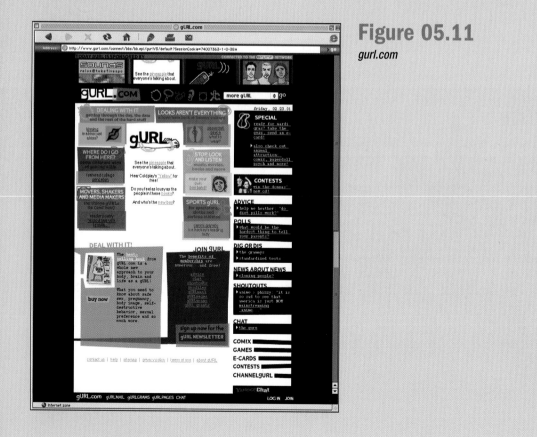

## Figure 05.11

*gurl.com*

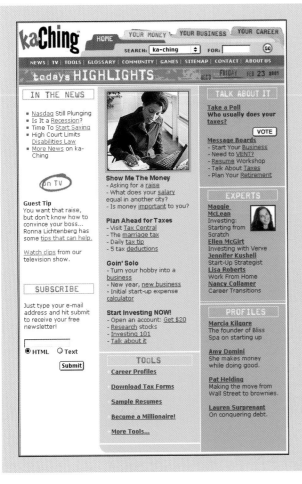

## Figure 05.12

*ka-ching.com*

# Techniques

The techniques of the Paper Bag Style are really none too technical. Most of the "craft" of this style occurs in the conceptual phase. After you have your idea, implementing this stuff is relatively straightforward. Having said that, let's look at some of the standard methods used to build paper bag sites.

# Paper Bag Textures

To get that crinkly, dirty, paper bag texture look, simply place a crinkly, dirty paper bag on a scanner and then scan it. (Actually, a crinkly, dirty piece of paper might work better.) I like to scan my paper at a low resolution (straight 72 dpi) and then enlarge it in Photoshop and save it as a very low-resolution jpeg. This effectively blurs and abstracts it so that it isn't so crisp. Saving it as a 16-color gif also works well. Do your own experimenting until you get something you like. Remember, the goal is a crinkly, worn effect, not a literal photographic match of the paper.

Save your bag-texture image at whatever dimensional size you like, and then simply call it into your page as a tiling background image. A 700×500-pixel image allows for a couple of good seam-showing tiles (**Figure 05.13**). You don't want your background image to be too small, or its tiling will form an ugly symmetrical pattern. Remember, the idea here is to escape symmetry. Another technique is to incorporate your paper texture into a nontiling foreground collage (**Figure 05.14**).

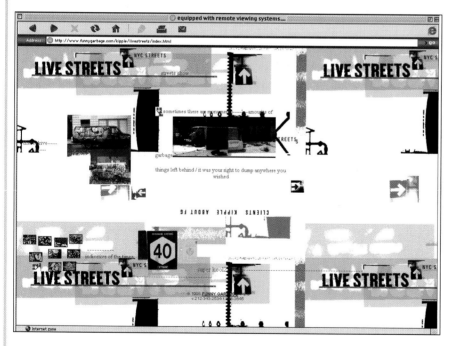

## Figure 05.13

*funnygarbage.com*

Hint: If you suddenly find yourself without a scanner, simply swipe a texture or two from the immense and ever-expanding airplane sickness bag virtual museum (**airsicknessbags.com**). I know I have.

## Figure 05.14

*stereomedia.net*

# Intentional Misalignment and Sloppy Boundaries

A tiling background texture is good, but a tiling background texture that intentionally leaves blank space for specific foreground images is even better. Build your entire page comp in Photoshop, being sure to keep your background image elements on one set of layers and your foreground image elements on a different set of layers.

How do you decide which elements go in the background image? Well, anything you don't want to tile should not go in the background image. It's also a good idea to limit your background image to greyscale so that its file size stays thin (it's already going to be 700×500 pixels, remember?). A general rule is that borders and textures go in the background, and colors, navigation elements, and featured items go in the foreground.

When designing the background border elements that will house your foreground images, make them skewed and misaligned however you like. Then let your foreground images sort of loosely disregard your borders (**Figure 05.02**). It will seem like things don't line up quite right, which is precisely what you want. (Warning: This technique drives neat-freak designers insane.)

Flatten your background layers into a single layer, and save that layer as a gif or jpeg. Save your individual foreground elements as gifs or jpegs. Then call your background image into your page as a tiling background, and use tables or CSS layers to position your foreground images on top of your background image as per your original comp layout. This positioning might take some trial and error, but it shouldn't prove too troublesome.

# Judicious Color Usage

Paper bag designers use color primarily for emphasis. When your entire page is in greyscale, it doesn't take a lot of color to attract attention (**Figure 05.01**). Use color for your links, navigational signposts, and feature elements. If the rest of your page is in greyscale, your color elements don't even have to be large in order to attract attention.

# The Nomadic Navigation Bar

Every web design book ever written says to choose a single location for your navigational menu and then stick with that same location throughout the site. If the same navigational menu changes location from one page to the next, your site visitor will be unable to recognize it as the same menu—despite the fact that the menu has exactly the same options, regardless of its location. Remember, users stupid. No can think.

Kipple throws this "fixed menu location" rule out the window. Their navigational menu hops around from page to page. Sometimes it appears at the very bottom of a page, and sometimes at the top. Sometimes it appears horizontally, and other times vertically. This novel nomadic navigational menu works well enough if you have only three or four options on your menu (Kipple has three). Otherwise, it's probably best to follow the general rule and stick with a fixed menu location.

The main mantra of the Paper Bag Style is "Just because you're not supposed to do it doesn't mean you can't." If you can figure out a way to make a good-looking "mistake" or a happy "irregularity," go for it. The rules are: There are no rules, as long as your approach works in context. Sometimes a site's context *demands* straightforward design. But other times, a site's context *demands* whimsical design. A truly versatile designer can execute either approach as needed.

## Sites Mentioned in This Chapter

http://www.funnygarbage.com/kipple/

http://www.p2output.com

http://www.vintage.levi.com

http://www.gurl.com

http://www.ka-ching.com

http://www.stereomedia.net

http://airsicknessbags.com

"There are two colors in my head. What was that you tried to say? Everything in its right place."

—Radiohead

**Figure 06.01**
*Piet Mondrian*

One of the major differences between the web and print is cost. Every printed page of paper costs money, but a web page is made of 0s and 1s. There is no paper; there is no ink. Sure, developing and hosting and bandwidth cost money, but once those costs are budgeted, disseminating hundreds of thousands of web pages every day is essentially free.

When designing a direct-mail brochure, you have to cram every last bit of information into a trifold piece of paper. But on the web, you can represent the same amount of information on a 10-page web site. Sadly, many corporations still don't get this. Most corporate home pages are cluttered to the max, with tons of different sections, all scrunched together and busily separated by borders galore. Front-page menus overflow with links to every single page on the site. Such a cluttered design approach is often unnecessary and almost always visually repellent. To feature every single thing is to actually feature nothing.

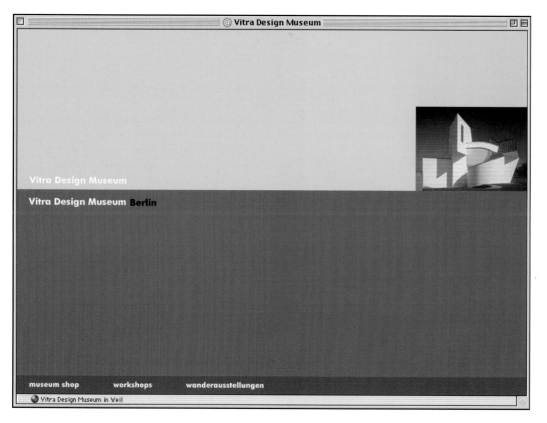

Figure 06.02

*design-museum.de*

Enter the Mondrian Poster Style of web design, named after the Swedish abstract expressionist Piet Mondrian (**Figure 06.01**). Mondrian poster sites take advantage of negative space and eschew borders (unlike Mondrian himself, who did use strong black borders). Mondrian poster sites instead use bold blocks of color to delineate sections (**Figure 06.02**). Some of these sites take this color block method to such extremes that they begin to resemble TV test-pattern color bars (**Figure 06.03**).

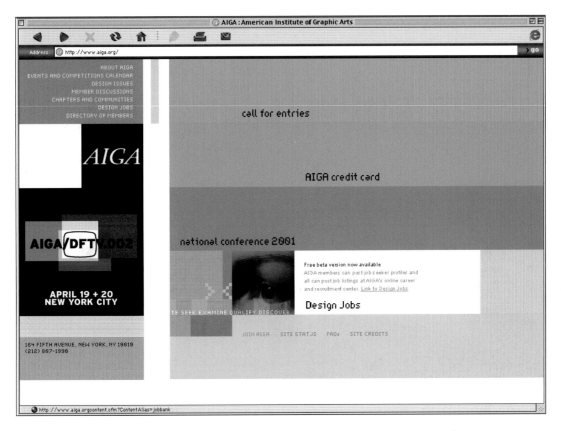

## Figure 06.03

*aiga.org*

Mondrian poster designers are full-screen designers. Aware that the entire browser window is their canvas, they do their best to fill it up—not with busy detail, but with color. Mondrian poster design embraces the minimalist aesthetic, but in a lush and gorgeous way rather than a stripped-down, scaled-back way. These sites do contain plenty of data and detail; it's just not all on the same page.

# Case Studies

Mondrian poster sites have an elegant, classy look. They are simple and bold. As such, this style is a natural for online museums, architecture firms, and online fashion catalogs. It's also perfect for classy restaurants, resorts, and nightclubs. I even envision it being used for a luxury automobile branding site. Any organization that wants to appear modern and smart is well-served by the Mondrian Poster Style. This style is probably weakest on sites that have deep hierarchies and lots of copy. Don't look for it on **wallstreetjournal.com** anytime soon.

# Vitra Design Museum and the Bauhaus Archive: Design Serving Design

What if you were hired to design a web site for a design museum? Which design style would you use? The web site couldn't be too in-your-face, or it would distract the visitors from the design objects featured in the museum. But neither could the site be too generic, because your clients and visitors are designers, and they expect something "designerly." The Vitra Design Museum and the Bauhaus Archive both chose to go with the Mondrian Poster Style for their web sites. It's the perfect style for such an "intentionally clean but not bland" assignment.

It's pretty easy for the front page of the Vitra Design Museum site to remain uncluttered at this initial level, because it has only a few links to display (**Figure 06.02**). Still, note the striking lack of border lines. The image to the right is framed by the solid teal section beneath it and by the browser window itself to its right. Note how open the page is. Nothing is scrunched into the top-left corner. The main visual element is actually one-third of the way down and to the far right. There is plenty of negative space but no white space; the entire page is full of color. And every single element on the page is in dialogue with the strong horizontal "line" formed by the intersection of the two main color blocks.

## Figure 06.04

*bauhaus.de*

The Bauhaus Archive front page is similarly open, while still managing to present the site's entire menu (**Figure 06.04**). When you move the mouse over an image link, the large color block on the bottom half of the page changes to the color of that particular section. This page starts in greyscale, and then suddenly it surprises you with bright, almost neon colors. This effect is quite arresting, yet it is achieved without Flash or any complicated programming.

On both museum sites, typography is crucial. Without borders, and with only horizontal color blocks, something has to take charge and convey the site's mood. The fonts are elegant, near-bold sans-serif—nothing playful or grungy.

Although these pages have no borders or lines, the various elements are still aligned with each other. With Mondrian poster sites, intentional alignment becomes all the more important, because there are no background grid patterns to help out the visitor. Without strong alignment, the objects on these pages would appear to float randomly in negative space. And randomness is the last thing this style seeks to invoke.

# 617: Fashion Jedi

617 is a portfolio site for a fashion industry design firm (**Figure 06.05**). 617 proves that your color blocks don't always have to be bright. There are just two background tones here—black and white. The bright colors are reserved for the section numbers and the portfolio work itself.

Note how the numbers go a bit below the dividing line. This anchors them to the strongest design element on the page (the horizontal intersection "line") and keeps them from floating around in space.

Again, note all the negative space, particularly above the numbers. The top-level navigation menu is refreshingly located at the bottom of the page. All that prime real estate in the top of the browser window is entirely wasted. And so what? The purpose of Mondrian poster design is to recontextualize the entire browser window into a single space. The old paradigm of the web page as a city block, where each lot must have a house on it, no longer applies. Mondrian poster design turns the entire browser window from Brooklyn into the Gulf of Mexico.

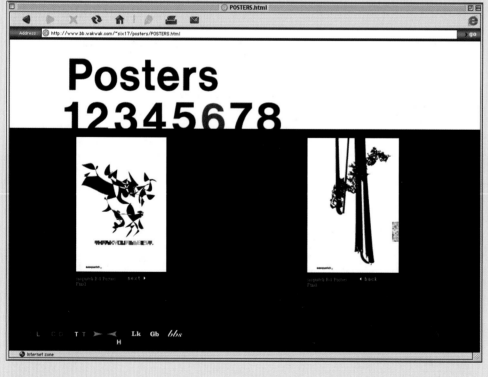

**Figure 06.05**

*bb.wakwak.com/~six17/*

# American Institute of Graphic Arts: Design Serving Designers

What if you were hired to design a web site exclusively for designers? Here again, the American Institute of Graphic Arts (AIGA) site chose to go with the Mondrian Poster Style (**Figure 06.06**). Everything is in its right place. The menu on the left keeps to itself. This menu actually has two subcolumns, yet nothing seems cluttered. The text and header block on the right maintain their own integrity. Note how the header block proceeds right to the edge of the browser window. The browser window itself is the "frame" for these blocks of color.

This page has strong vertical columns of information, yet without any vertical lines or borders. Again, the trick is alignment. The black block on the left side splits the left menu column into two subcolumns. The subcolumns then proceed in orderly alignment according to the color blocks above them. Does this page have strongly defined sections? Sure. They just aren't surrounded by borders.

For the sake of readability, the designers of the AIGA site opted to leave the body copy on a white background. So this page is not totally saturated with color, but it's still mighty colorful. The color blocks might seem like mere abstract design, but they actually serve to vertically and horizontally establish the sections of the page. Furthermore, the color of the header block ties in with the site's overall navigation scheme.

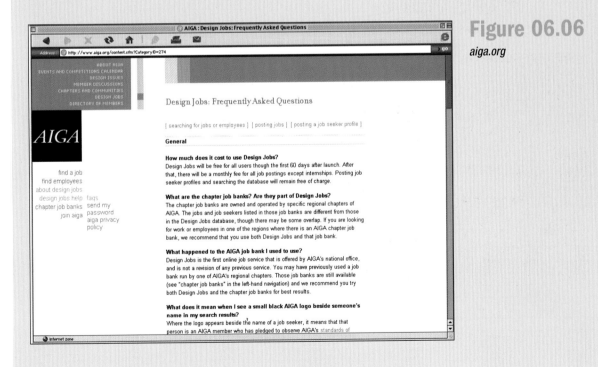

## Figure 06.06

*aiga.org*

# Lundstrom Architecture: Built to Impress

The purpose of the Lundstrom Architecture site is to make Lundstrom and Associates look both organized and creative (**Figure 06.07**). Prospective clients visiting this site want to be assured that they aren't throwing their money away on an amateurish firm incapable of handling budgets and meeting deadlines. But they also want to hire a firm with creative vision—a firm that thinks out of the box. Juxt Interactive's site for Lundstrom fulfills those two requirements and more.

The Lundstrom site uses color blocks, but this time they aren't all rectangular. The arches and angles of this page's layout complement the lines of the buildings that are displayed. In a departure from the classic Mondrian Poster Style, single-pixel lines are also used, mostly to connect text links with the images to which they refer.

There are three full menus on this tiny page. Yet the navigation is intuitive and usable. Space is saved via rollover functions. All six buildings on the "hands" menu couldn't be displayed simultaneously on this page without taking up too much room. Instead, mousing over a building's name causes that building's image to appear in the space to the right of the hands. Clicking the building's name then leads to a new page at the site's next level, with more information on that building.

This is not the only tight Mondrian poster site that Juxt Interactive has built, but it remains one of their best. Juxt's founder, Todd Purgason, is obsessed with seeing just how much information he can fit into a limited space while still keeping his design navigable and clean. When it comes to pushing this style to its limits, Juxt Interactive is the Industrial Light and Magic of the Mondrian Poster Style.

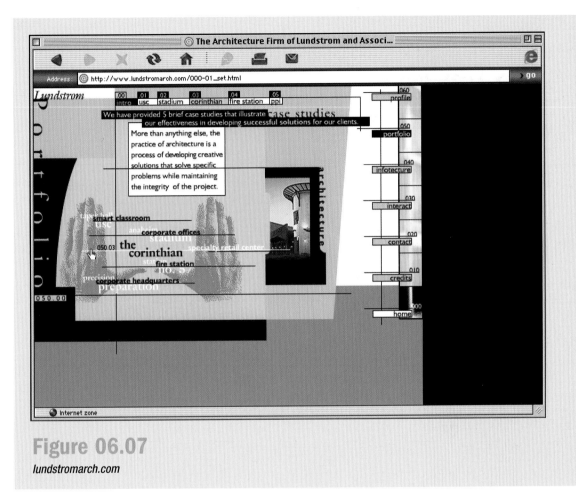

**Figure 06.07**

*lundstromarch.com*

# Techniques

The techniques of the Mondrian Poster Style have more to do with layout philosophy and less to do with any particular piece of software or code. For example, the Lundstrom Architecture site and the Vitra Design Museum site both have Flash and HTML versions, and this style works equally well in either version. Once you understand the basic design principles involved, implementing this look is often a matter of course.

# Holistic Browser Window Design

The most defining characteristic of the Mondrian Poster Style is that it fills the entire browser window with at least two different blocks of color. Lots of sites fill the entire browser window with one block of color. It's called the page's background color. But at least two distinct color blocks are required for the Mondrian Poster effect.

## The Frames Solution

Most Mondrian poster sites use frames, although there are other equally valid approaches. For instance, you could lay out your page in a table and define the background color for each table data cell like so: **<td bgcolor="ff3300">**. Or, better yet, you could lay out your page using CSS **<div>**s and define the background color for each **<div>** in an external style sheet, like so: **DIV { background-color: ff3300}**. But here I examine the classic frames-based approach.

To get two big color blocks via the frames method, simply build two pages, define each page's background color, and then call the two pages into your frameset. This method works well, because it allows you to take advantage of "liquid" page layout by soft-coding the height of certain frames as percentages.

For example, here is the source code for the 617 poster page (**Figure 06.05**):

```
<HTML>
<HEAD>
 <TITLE>POSTERS.html</TITLE>
</HEAD>
<FRAMESET ROWS="184,56%,60"border=0 framespacing=0 frameborder=0>
        <FRAME SRC="POSTERSTOP.html" NAME="POSTERSTOP" SCROLLING=NO >

        <FRAMESET COLS="139,70%">
        <FRAME SRC="POSTERSLEFT.html" NAME="POSTERSLEFT" SCROLLING=NO >
        <FRAME SRC="POSTERSRIGHT.html" NAME="POSTERSRIGHT"SCROLLING=NO >
        </FRAMESET>

        <FRAME SRC="../BOTTOM/FRAMEBOTTOM.html" NAME="POSTERBOTTOM" SCROLLING=NO >
        </FRAMESET>
<NOFRAMES>
<BODY>
????
</BODY>
</NOFRAMES>
</FRAMESET>
</HTML>
```

The first horizontal row is set at 184 pixels high for the frame that contains the numbers. Then, the frame that contains the actual portfolio work is set at 56%. It could just as well have been set at *, because it fills up the remaining window space after the other two horizontal frames have taken up their hard-coded space. Finally, the bottom menu frame is set at 60 pixels high. Note that all scrolling is turned off to avoid the unsightly appearance of browser scrollbars in the middle of the page.

The 56% frame is then subdivided into two horizontal frames—one hard-coded and one resizable as a percentage—thus creating a static left margin in this middle frame. There are other ways to make such a margin, but this was the solution the designers chose here.

Now the page resizes vertically in proportion to the amount of space left in the browser window. Personally, I would have allowed vertical scrolling in the middle frame, because at 800×600, some of the art gets cropped by the bottom menu. But you get the general idea.

## The Full-Screen Flash Solution

Joshua Davis's Once Upon A Forest is a brilliant example of purely artistic Mondrian poster design (**Figure 06.08**). The site is always divided into two frames, with the bottom navigation frame laid out in tables. The top frame always contains a Flash file with its width and height set to 100%. Consequently, the Flash art expands or contracts to fill the visitor's entire screen, regardless of the screen's resolution. Because Flash is vectorized, all line art and text scales gracefully without pixelating. And because these pieces are mostly abstract, stretching them a bit vertically or horizontally usually doesn't harm them.

**Figure 06.08**

*once-upon-a-forest.com*

## The Fixed-Size Solution

A third solution to holistic screen design is to place your content in a fixed area and then surround that fixed area with color blocks that complement it (**Figure 06.09**). A fixed area surrounded by white looks scrunched and accidental, as if the designer forgot to consider what the page might look like in a bigger browser window. But a fixed area surrounded by complementary color blocks tells the visitor, "I realize your browser is oversized for my focus area, so I've given you some attractive negative space to look at during your visit."

## The Pop-Up Window Solution

Frustrated at the unknown browser window size conundrum, more and more designers are building entire sites in pop-up windows. A site's front page automatically launches a fixed-size pop-up window in which the remainder of the site is viewed. This solution makes site designing less complicated, simply because you know the size of the browser window, since you created it.

The problem with this solution is, if someone wants to link to a page on your site other than the front page, they bypass your pop-up resize mojo, and then you're back to the unknown window size conundrum. Of course, if your entire site is one giant Flash file, no one will be able to link to an internal page anyway, so go ahead and fiddle while Rome burns. Pop up, up, and away!

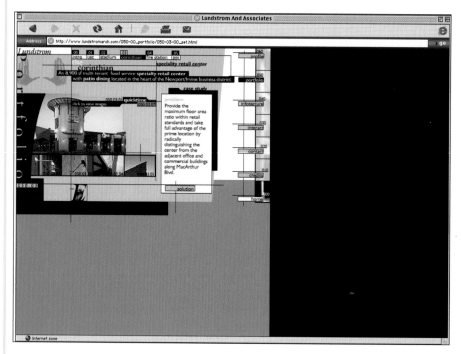

## Figure 06.09

*lundstromarch.com at 1024×768*

# Navigation Integrated into Overall Page Design

Every web page needs navigation elements and a defining visual metaphor. Mondrian poster designers figure, "Why not kill two birds with one stone and use the navigation elements as the defining visual metaphor?" Such a solution is brilliant and very nonprint. What print designer would turn a magazine's page numbers into a defining visual metaphor? (OK, David Carson. Who else?) Yet on the web, it makes good intuitive sense to integrate navigation into a page's overall layout.

At 617, large link numbers become the page's key visual element (**Figure 06.05**). This is a clever wink from a design firm whose name consists entirely of numbers.

The core level of the Vitra Design Museum site looks like a stack of colored construction paper (**Figure 06.10**). Choose a section from the top menu bar, and that section's colored construction paper "rises" to the top of the stack for viewing. But notice what happens to the menu bar. In this case, the blue of the construction paper seems to permeate the menu bar itself.

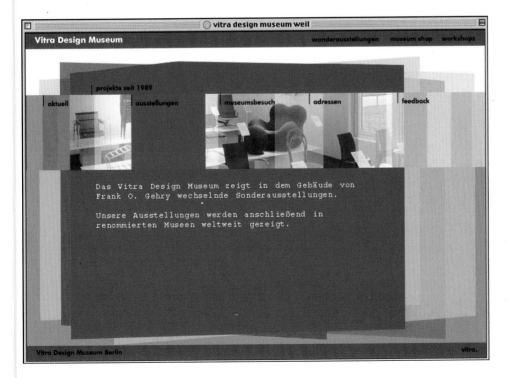

## Figure 06.10

*design-museum.de*

It's nothing new to have color-coded sections. Typically, it works like this: The "contact us" text on a site's menu bar might be blue, and then every page in the "contact us" section has some blue in it. But the Vitra site takes this "color locator" trick to ingenious extremes. Not only are the menu and page similarly color-coded, but they are actually adjoined and spatially modified.

At both Vitra and 617, entire visual metaphors arise out of the necessity of web site navigation. Rather than view navigational menus as a cluttering menace, Mondrian poster designers have embraced this "constraint" of the medium and are using navigation menus to drive creative design solutions.

# Intentional Color Palette

It goes without saying that every web site should be built with color coordination in mind. But this is especially true of Mondrian poster sites, where color plays such an important role. There are basically two approaches to Mondrian poster color usage: same hue/different saturation, and same saturation/different hue.

Once Upon A Forest uses the same hue/different saturation approach. Every month, the site features a single hue. One month, the site might be predominantly green. Yet within that same green hue are varying degrees of saturation—from muted green to bright green. For help

with choosing an appropriate palette for this approach, visit Joshua Davis's very useful color "machine" at **http://www.cyphen.com**.

A more standard solution is to use different hues but make sure they are all the same saturation (**Figure 06.03**). You don't want a muted blue and a bright red. This same saturation/different hue approach works well for sites with multiple sections, because it's much easier to remember "the red section versus the green section" than it is to remember "the aqua section versus the teal section."

Versatile and professionally elegant, the Mondrian Poster Style is a handy arrow to have in your professional design quiver. Using just HTMinimaLism and Mondrian poster, 90% of the commercial web could conceivably be built. Although it's initially challenging to think about designing without borders, once you've made the transition, you may never go back.

# Sites Mentioned in This Chapter

http://www.design-museum.de

http://www.aiga.org

http://www.bauhaus.de

http://www.bb.wakwak.com/~six17/

http://www.lundstromarch.com

http://www.once-upon-a-forest.com

http://www.cyphen.com

"I'm a street-walking cheetah with a heart full of napalm. I'm the runaway son of a nuclear A-bomb. I am the world's forgotten boy. The one who's searching to destroy."

—Iggy Pop

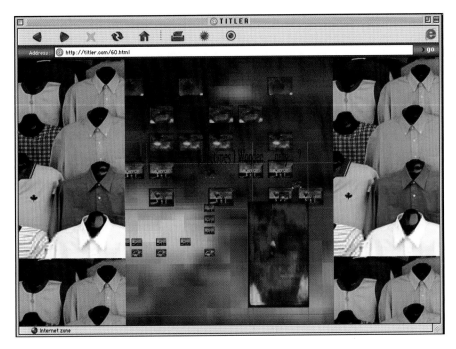

**Figure 07.01**

*titler.com*

When they hear the words "punk rock," most people envision screaming, unkempt youngsters with brightly colored Mohawks and bicycle-chain jewelry. This connotation is unfortunate, because these superficial external fashions have little to do with the true essence of punk. So before I begin unraveling the mysteries of the Pixelated Punk Rock Style of web design, I'd best spend a little time redefining punk proper.

Punk is less a late-'70s musical movement and more of an attitude. John Coltrane's post-1964 "free jazz" was punk. The Velvet Underground's *White Light/White Heat* album was punk. Even Marcel Duchamp's ostentatiously entitled urinal was punk.

Punk is a playful (psychotic?) tweaking of the ridiculous and established norms of society, but to such a degree as to be deemed downright wrong. Punk is like a prank that's gone too far, yet hasn't even begun. Punk is intense self-destruction as protest, so much so that it can't help but spill over and destroy others. Punk bothers "normal" people.

It follows, then, that the Pixelated Punk Rock Style of design is intentionally off-putting, user-unfriendly, disorienting, and annoying (if not downright emotionally disturbing). At a pixelated punk rock site, a surfer is rarely sure where he is, or why, or how to proceed. Sometimes he's not even sure where his browser window ends and the web site proper begins. He might even feel like his CPU is melting. At a pixelated punk rock site, a surfer is merely a rat in the site designer's maze (**Figure 07.01**).

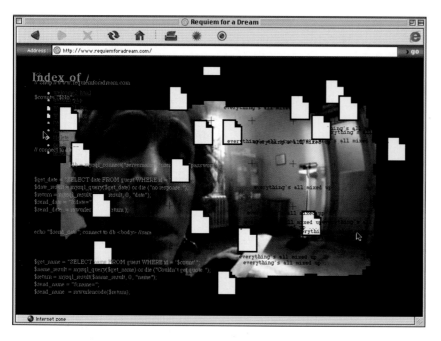

**Figure 07.02**

*requiemforadream.com*

Having defined pixelated punk rock as such, the next logical question is, "What commercial applications, if any, could such a web design style possibly have?" The answer is, "Very few—so far." I do examine one commercial example of this style— a promotional web site for the seriously disturbing experimental film *Requiem for a Dream* (**Figure 07.02**).

Other than that, useful applications of this style remain to be pioneered. I can think of at least three possible commercial applications for this style:

- A smear site for a corporate rival. "Use company X's inferior product, and you might have the following horrible experience. Click here."
- An "Alice in Wonderland" children's game site, where nothing is what it seems.

- A "find your way out of the maze" site where the goal is to escape the overwhelming disorientation and find your way back to normal.

With so few documented commercial uses for the Pixelated Punk Rock Style, why am I giving it its own chapter? Because you might find a use for it that I have not yet envisioned. And because whether you use this style or not, these pixelated punk rock sites will cause you to think about the web in a whole new way.

# A Brief Orientation in Disorientation

As a computer user, you've come to expect your computer to act a certain way. Your machine beeps when you do something wrong; it displays red stop signs and blinking warnings when you click out of bounds; it spits machine-code gobbledygook and distorted images back at you when things really take a nosedive. If you're on a PC, you often get ejected from Windows and dumped back into DOS when things go really wrong. In short, you've learned what your computer looks like and sounds like when it malfunctions. You've been conditioned to expect certain behavior from a broken machine.

Pixelated punk rock web designers take your conditioned expectations and exploit them. These designers won't actually crash your machine (at least, not intentionally). Instead, they build their sites to make your machine look as if it's crashing. Or they build their sites to make your machine look as if it has a mind of its own. Visiting one of these sites is like going to an earthquake movie where the entire theater shakes (a la "rumble-rama" in the '50s, or so they tell me).

Ironically, pixelated punk rock is the most "media aware" of all the styles in this book. In order to make something seem broken, you have to have a pretty good understanding of how that something works. You can't intentionally be unusable without first understanding the parameters of usability. Consequently, pixelated punk rock designers have thought a lot about the core elements of the web browsing experience.

Web browsing is not really a seamless, integrated experience. As you surf the web, you are actually receiving and processing two different types of information. The first type comes from the web sites you visit. It usually exists within the browser window. The second type of information comes from your browser software itself. The loading status message at the bottom of your browser, the scrollbar, the URLs that appear in your address field, the pop-up error messages telling you that such-and-such a site cannot be found—all these "signals" come not from the sites you visit, but from the browser software itself.

Think of the site-derived information as "immediate information" and the browser-derived information as "meta-information." Note, however, that the web site itself actually "drives" both types of information. If a site's page is long, that causes the browser to scroll. If a site takes a long time to load, that causes the browser to display download information. Using JavaScript, a site can even command the browser to display a pop-up window message.

As a rule, you tend to trust the meta-information from the browser more than you trust the immediate information from the site. Any old shmo can cause pink animated bats to zing around his web site in shocking DHTML fury. But that's just something happening on that person's silly personal web site. Yet when you get an error message from Internet Explorer telling you that your memory is running low, hey, that's like a message from Bill Gates himself! (And everybody trusts Bill Gates, right?) Such an error message from the browser suddenly involves you, because you are no longer merely peering through a window into someone else's broken world. Now you've been made responsible for mending your own broken world.

It is this familiarity with and trust of technology that pixelated punk rockers exploit, and for a variety of reasons. **titler.com** is Dada—disorienting you to mock your expectations of the norm, and laughing all the while. **day-dream.com** is abstract art—disorienting you because disorientation looks cool. **dream7.com** is surrealistic—speaking to you in some primordial Jungian language, the very nature of which is inherently disorienting. And **requiemforadream.com** is moralistic—disorienting you so that you viscerally experience other people's disorientation and thus empathize with them.

Disorientation—it's not just for breakfast anymore!

# Case Studies

What follows is an examination of some popular disorientation methods used by pixelated punk rock designers. Some examples are merely playful, and others are positively jarring. They all have one thing in common—an overt attempt to undermine the user's expectations.

# Fake Malfunction

The most obvious way to disorient a surfer is to send him an authoritative message that something is wrong. With surfers getting more and more wily these days, a simple JavaScript alert box saying "I've erased your entire hard drive" just ain't gonna cut it anymore. Nope, serious appearance of actual machine malfunction is required.

Enter day-dream.com. From the site's core page, a pop-up window appears. It looks like an ordinary Netscape download window, with a status bar showing you the progress of the download (**Figure 07.03**). But move the mouse over the window, and a siren goes off, causing the status bar to curl up in a very abnormal way. Clicking the Cancel button causes strange clicking noises to occur. The longer you wait, the more disheveled the fake download window becomes. Letters start floating and spinning, you hear more weird noises, and finally, as you approach 95% complete, the entire window seems to totally fall apart (**Figure 07.04**). Then suddenly you are looped back to 23% complete status, and the whole process starts over again.

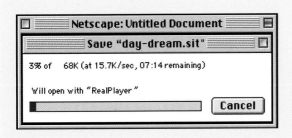

## Figure 07.03

*3%*

## Figure 07.04

*95%*

This fake pop-up window actually contains a Shockwave file with various programmed interactive behaviors. It looks like a standard Netscape download window, but looks are deceiving. In a way, it's kind of like those banner ad gifs that use fake scrollbars to get you to click on them. Except at day-dream, you're not being sold anything (other than a disorienting experience).

The pranksters at **hi-res.net** use this fake malfunction element on two of their sites. At **soulbath.com**, you are asked, "Want to play a game? Click on screen once." What follows is a noninteractive tic-tac-toe game that you immediately lose, because you're not allowed to make any moves. Then you're forwarded to what looks like a normal e-commerce site, which suddenly melts before your eyes, replete with intermittent cryptic machine-code error messages, an ominous ASCII-art scull, and elongated/corrupt image blips. From the meltdown screen, you see a series of JavaScript alert box messages, but before you can answer them by clicking OK, the site clicks OK for you. Finally, all this movement stops, and you're presented with one last alert box that says, "Continue? I mean, you don't have much of a choice…". Finally, you are allowed to click the OK button yourself, and you are ushered to your destination.

How is all this mayhem accomplished? Some screens look like command-line interfaces, other screens look like HTML pages, and still other screens look like JavaScript browser alert messages. In fact, the entire sequence is just a single streaming Flash file. The alert boxes merely appear to pop up. They are actually just interactive elements within the Flash animation. And the apparent meltdown of the e-commerce site? It's all created in Flash to simulate a major machine malfunction.

Hi-res employs this Flash meltdown trick again at their brilliant requiemforadream.com, the promotional site for the Darren Aronofsky film of the same name. This time, the infomercial web site of motivational speaker Tappy Tibbons appears to freak out and collapse (**Figure 07.05**). In the context of the *Requiem* site, this meltdown simulates the decaying mental state of Sara, a diet pill addict who wins a guest appearance on the Tappy Tibbons show. Thus, a design element that was playful at soulbath.com becomes sinister and cautionary at requiemforadream.com.

Figure 07.05

requiemforadream.com

# Rigged Navigation

You've already encountered one example of rigged navigation at soulbath.com. You're told, "Continue? I mean, you don't have much of a choice…", and the only option you're given is OK. Later at soulbath, you're presented with a similar faux-choice, "Continue? y/n." If you choose no, you're served a pseudo-JavaScript alert that says, "Sorry, that was actually a rhetorical question." You then see yet another "OK" option, which forwards you down the "yes" path. Such navigation is rigged. It seems like you're in control of your experience, when actually you're being led down a path of the web designer's own devising.

A wonderful example of rigged navigation occurs at **e13.com**. Unlike soulbath, where only a few navigational elements are rigged, e13's entire navigational scheme is rigged.

e13 uses HTML forms to navigate. You're asked to enter a keyword into a blank and click Enter. At first, a valid keyword is supplied for you, which takes you to a functional page of the site. But after that, if you want to visit different pages of the site, you have to make up your own keyword. No matter what keyword you choose, you are taken to a page that says, in effect, "Sorry, page not found" (**Figure 07.06**). Here, you are offered a single random link to another legitimate page of the site. And so it goes. In order to visit a new page of the site, you have to type in yet another made-up keyword (knowing it will be wrong) in order to get to the error message page and discover the next random link. You know you've seen the entire site only when the random link suggestions begin repeating themselves. Even then, you're not quite sure.

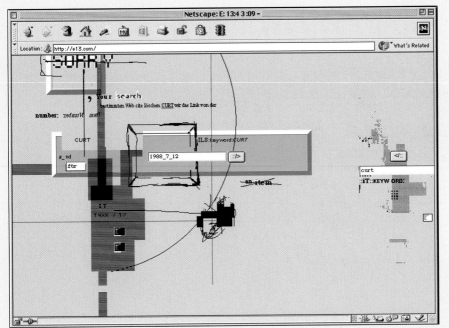

**Figure 07.06**

*e13.com*

So here again you have an example of an interface that appears to be quite user-empowering (you can type in any word you want, after all!) but that is actually a disorienting rig to limit user power. If e-13's navigational scheme "works," you'll imagine yourself as a code breaker and proceed to explore every nook and cranny of this site with the illicit glee of a hacker exploring a secret database. If e-13's navigational scheme fails, you'll get bored and leave quicker than you can say, "Nobody's fool." Ah, art.

# Missing or Misleading Signposts

Like Alice's Wonderland, things are rarely what they seem at pixelated punk rock sites. You might stumble across an occasional signpost letting you know where you are, but it is usually misleading. The designer's goal is to remove the surfer's control of the experience. If I know where I am, where I've been, and where I'm going, I'm not disoriented. So pixelated punk rock sites rarely have navigation menus, and when they do, they are so cryptic as to be virtually useless.

Text links rarely indicate where they lead. A link that says, "I see London, I see France," might lead to a poem that begins, "I saw a pig's eye floating down the frothy gutters of Rue Perdu." Or, more confusing still, there are no text links at all, only image links.

Sometimes the links *are* related to the content to which they lead, but the relationships are so cryptic and subjective that you are forced to rethink your entire perspective on the two things being linked. For instance, at dream7.com, the text link "rake across sand" (**Figure 07.07**) leads to an interactive Flash animation where mousing over a blank area causes abstract shapes and sounds to materialize (**Figure 07.08**). Without the text link, this would have been just another abstract interactive animation. With the text link, you imagine yourself raking sand. You are forced by virtue of association to perceive the animation differently.

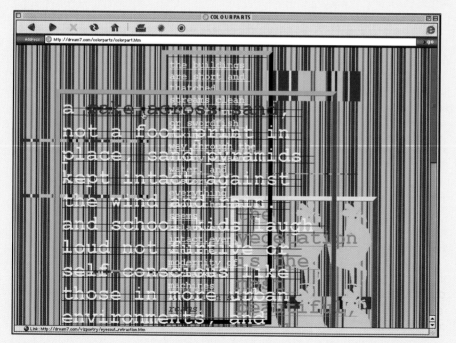

**Figure 07.07**

*Raking text*

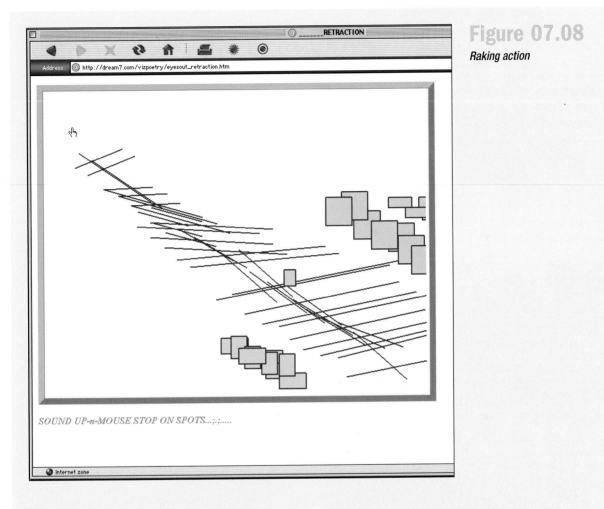

**Figure 07.08**

*Raking action*

Perhaps there is a commercial application here in the midst of all this disorientation. The web has the power to juxtapose two different things and present them in such a way that the surfer is forced to construct a new relationship between them. A recent print ad campaign that operates on this same principle is the "Dodge Different" campaign. A series of firecrackers are lined up next to a stick of dynamite, a series of simple fishing hooks are lined up next to an intricate fly-fishing lure, and so on. There are only two words in the entire campaign. Thus, all the attention is shifted to the unlabeled, seemingly unrelated objects. The ad forces

you to connect these objects in a way that adds value to them and thus adds value to the Dodge product. This is abstract branding at its best. Not once does a truck ever appear in the entire ad campaign.

It would seem that simply by proceeding page by page at these pixelated punk rock sites, you should eventually be able to get through them from beginning to end in a semi-orderly fashion. Alas, this is not so. titler.com foils you by using randomly generated links. titler.com has fewer than 100 discrete pages, but page 50 does not always lead to page 51. Indeed, a single link on any given page might lead to 60 different pages at any given time. This random linking is accomplished by having all links lead to a single address, which then randomly and instantaneously forwards you to another page. Try backtracking to the previous page, and you actually wind up backtracking to the interim forwarding address, which immediately spits you forward to yet another random page. Thus, even the path you followed into the site seems to have shifted behind you. A punk rock raven has come and eaten your digital bread crumbs, and you are left stranded in the cyber-wilds.

To make matters worse (or better, depending on whose side you're on), several pages at titler share the same images and animations. One page calls an image in as a full-page element. Another page calls the same image in and sets it off in a corner. And some pages are really just framesets that call in multiple pages (**Figure 07.09**)—pages that later appear on their own outside the framed environment. Surf titler.com long enough, and you eventually stumble upon a page you've already visited. But more often than not, you'll stumble upon a page that has elements from pages you've already visited, but that is not the same. It's kind of like having deja vu while you're dreaming. Now how much would you pay!

**Figure 07.09**

*titler.com*

requiemforadream.com also buries its sign-posts. There are two main ways to proceed through the *Requiem* site. One way is to follow the story of Sara, and the other is to follow the story of her son, Harry. At the major fork in the site, where you choose between these two characters, you are presented with a white void. Only by mous-ing over the hidden Flash file can you see anything. What you do see gradually fades in and out as you run your cursor over it, so some parts of the "big picture" always remain hidden.

The Flash file reveals the figures of a man and a woman. Mousing over either figure causes it to glow red (**Figure 07.10**). Clicking the woman leads down Sara's story path. Clicking the man leads down Harry's story path. But the entire Flash collage is so shift-ing and fractured that you are lucky to find even a single link, much less both links. It's only after revisiting the site and finding yourself on a new story path that you realize there was a fork.

Diverging from these two main story paths are all sorts of subpaths. For instance, Sara begins hallucinating that her refrigerator is talking to her. If you click the fridge, one type of immediate breakdown occurs. If you try to control your willpower and avoid clicking the fridge, things get crazier and crazier, and then another kind of breakdown occurs (**Figure 07.02**).

Throughout the site, there is no clear map saying, "Pick path A, B, or C." In that sense, requiemforadream.com simulates life. In real life, important life-changing decisions are often made without any clear understanding of their future consequences. Just pray you don't make the decisions these characters make. I count at least six different possible "endings" to the *Requiem* site narrative, each one more terrifying than the last.

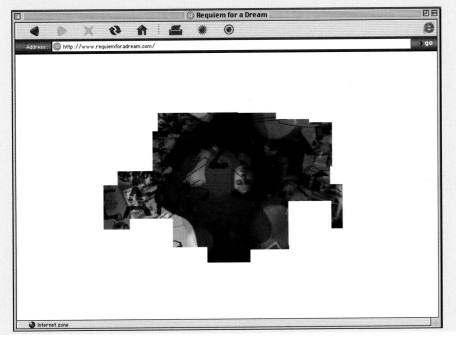

**Figure 07.10**

*requiemforadream.com*

# Perpetual Motion and Noise

Another hallmark of the Pixelated Punk Rock Style is the use of lots of motion and noise. I would say "audio" or "music," but more often it is merely beeps and blurps and static accompanying a barrage of whirling, spinning, and blipping animation. Usability experts caution against using a lot of motion on a page, because the eye is immediately drawn to it. Some folks claim this has to do with saber-toothed tigers chasing hunter/gatherers many moons ago. I disagree, but whatever the explanation, humans do tend to focus on moving images.

So what better way to disorient a surfer than by giving him not one but dozens of animations, all moving in and out of synch, accompanied by various electronic audio blurts at distorted volume levels? In keeping with the "lack of user control" theme, pixelated punk rock sites rarely offer a

"mute" option. day-dream wins the award for most massive assault on the senses, using a combination of Shockwave and animated gifs to simulate silicon meltdown (**Figure 07.11**). If anyone ever did a "This is your computer. This is your computer on drugs" campaign, day-dream would be the "computer on drugs" poster child.

titler.com also employs all manner of animated media—so much so that at least one element on any given titler page is always moving. Unlike day-dream, titler uses actual music as background audio—mostly soothing '30s string ballads. But don't let the mellow tunes fool you. The goal of these tame selections is usually some strange, ironic disconnect. One particular lilting melody provides a disturbing soundtrack to a slow-motion collage of violent explosions. On another titler page, buildings are demolished before your eyes (and beneath your cursor) as a melancholy crooner sings, "Let it go. Let it go." titler's audio and images are often intentionally at odds, leaving you to reconcile the incongruities.

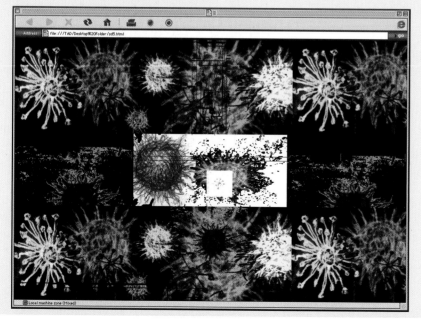

**Figure 07.11**

*day-dream.com*

# Unorthodox Image Cropping, Enlargement, and Subject Matter

In addition to using abstract line art, pixelated punk rock sites often incorporate jpeg photographs. The goal is to take a semirecognizable real-world scene and present it in a distorted way. Sometimes you're shown only a part of the picture. At titler, a waving human arm takes on an eerie birdlike quality because the image is cropped to focus you on the arm's movement, diverting your attention from the fact that this is a picture of someone's appendage (**Figure 07.12**). Extreme close-ups of faces cropped off-center, extreme close-ups of signs and buildings from irregular angles—all these images are calculated to "stand you on your head," to distort your perception, to disorient you.

As if strange cropping weren't punk enough, many of these images are further mutated by drastic enlargement, which leads to pixelation. Sometimes the images are so pixelated that they look like abstract digital mosaics (**Figure 07.13**). Other times, the images are still recognizable, but just barely. All of this pixelation adds yet another layer of digital distortion to the mix—the ghost of Georges Seurat in the machine.

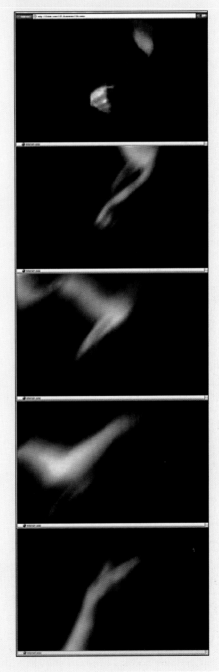

**Figure 07.12**

*titler.com*

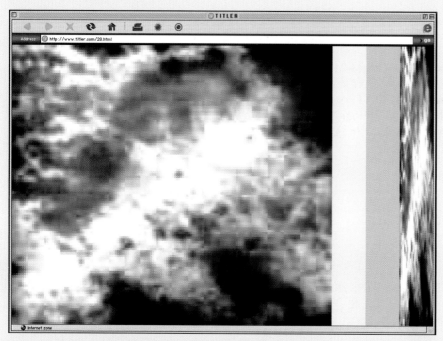

**Figure 07.13**

*titler.com*

**Figure 07.14**

*titler.com*

Finally, to add further insult to your already decaying sensibilities, most of these images are of banal, seemingly random subjects. Streets, buildings, signs, and hallways all regularly appear at pixelated punk rock sites, but close inspection usually reveals no intentional subject matter whatsoever. It's as if someone just aimlessly walked along with a camera, pointing and clicking at random. What better way to introduce a feeling of disconnect than by featuring images with no "point" at all (**Figure 07.14**)? The implication is that such banal subject matter has as much right to be considered art as any Ansel Adams or Rembrandt. I'm not saying I agree with this relativistic, post-modern assertion. I'm just explaining the style.

# Techniques

Pixelated punk rock has its own unique array of techniques, all geared toward manipulating the conventional expectations of the web as a medium. These techniques in and of themselves are not especially disorienting; there's nothing that avant-garde about full-screen layouts or mouseover functions. It's the unorthodox implementation of these techniques that invokes the mayhem.

# Rogue Multimedia

A CD sounds different than vinyl. Digital TV looks different than analog TV. Film looks different than video. Each medium has its own particular "feel." The same is true on the web. A Flash animation moves differently than a QuickTime movie, which moves differently than an animated gif. An all-Flash web page loads differently than a standard HTML web page. A Shockwave file responds differently to a mouseover than DHTML does.

Pixelated punk rockers, being media-hyperconscious, are aware of these differences in web technology behavior. Moreover, they play on these differences, making Flash pages that seem like standard HTML pages (until they melt), Shockwave animations that seem like animated gifs (until they interact), and QuickTime movies that seem like Flash animations (until they render bitmapped image motion like a Super-8 film camera).

At titler, Flash animations are often used as individual elements within a regular HTML layout. Most Flash pages these days are designed entirely within Flash, and then a sparse HTML "holder page" is used to contain the entire Flash animation. But at titler, Flash is used as an animated gif would be. The results are unusual, because what seems to be a mere animated gif is enabled with interactive properties that only Flash has. On one page, a mouseover causes a building to crumble, while a mouseoff causes the same building to rewind and "rebuild" itself. Such functionality is simply not possible with standard DHTML. And even if it were, the motion's "feel" would not be the same.

Whereas titler uses Flash within HTML, requiemforadream.com simulates HTML with Flash. So when *Requiem*'s fake HTML pages begin to melt, warp, and do things no normal HTML page could ever do (**Figure 07.05**), you are taken by surprise. If you knew you were viewing a Flash animation, you might expect such full-screen, cross-boundary movements and behaviors. But the page fools you because it doesn't look like what you expect a Flash page to look like.

Few web surfers could consciously articulate the differences between HTML and Flash, but repetitive surfing has conditioned them to expect certain behaviors from web pages that look certain ways. They are unconsciously aware of these behavioral expectations. Disrupt these expectations, and most surfers will react in emotional, nonrational ways.

I have not even begun to discuss QuickTime, Shockwave, RealVideo, RealAudio, DHTML movement, animated gifs, Java applets, and so on. Pixelated punk rockers are infamous for mixing and matching any and all available web technologies in order to disrupt surfer expectations. The trick is to set up your visitors to expect one thing and then deliver something beyond their expectations. Remember how the *Wizard of Oz* starts off in black and white and then kicks into color when Dorothy touches down in Munchkin Land? Remember how hyper-bright that color seems in comparison to the beginning of the film? Such is the desired effect of rogue multimedia.

# Full-Screen Control

If you are trying to take over someone's computer and disrupt his entire world view, you can't do it all scrunched up in the top-left corner of the browser window. Nor can you do it from some tiny pop-up window. That's why pixelated punk rock sites fill the entire browser window at all times. Pixelated punk rockers don't want surfers to peer into their sites. Pixelated punk rockers want surfers to be surrounded by their sites.

One way to cover the entire screen is with a tiling background image. If the image happens to be animated, all the better.

Another way to cover the entire screen is to build a page containing multiple frames (**Figure 07.09**). In a sense, you've served your visitor several pages at once. Each page is free to pursue its own independent path, leaving the other pages unchanged in the browser window. To create an exit from this framed environment, just include a **target=top** attribute to whichever link you want to act as your "frame escape" link, and your visitor will be returned to the standard "single-page" environment.

Another way to cover the entire screen is to use Flash. Because Flash animations are vector-based, you can fill an entire page with a Flash file simply by specifying its width and height attributes as percentages rather than pixels. (To fill the entire screen, just specify 100% width and 100% height.) If your Flash animation includes a bitmapped image, such enlargement will cause blurring and pixelation (**Figure 07.15**). Excellent!

**Figure 07.15**

*titler.com*

There is even a way to make a normal jpeg or gif cover the entire screen. Just place the image you want to enlarge at the very top of your page, making sure your **<body>** tag includes the attributes **leftmargin=0 topmargin=0 marginwidth=0 marginheight=0**. Then, simply set the image's height and width attributes to 100%. In Netscape, this causes a vertical scrollbar to appear. (Why Netscape thinks that 100% of the viewable window actually means 102% of the viewable window is beyond me, but there you are.) The way to lose the scrollbar is to create a workaround frameset that looks like this:

```
<frameset rows="100%,*" cols="*" border="0" framespacing="0" frameborder="NO">
 <frame name="content" src="mypage.html" scrolling="no" marginwidth="0"
marginheight="0" frameborder="0" noresize framespacing="0">
 <frame name="un_used" src="blank.html" scrolling="no" marginwidth="0"
marginheight="0" frameborder="0" noresize framespacing="0">
</frameset>
```

where **mypage.html** is the name of the actual page you want to call in. Here Netscape requires you to create a blank page (blank.html in the preceding code) and call it into a second frame that has no dimensions. Netscape forces you to use two frames because it correctly assumes that no one in their right mind would create a frameset containing only one frame. And Netscape would be right, had its previous bug not caused you to need to do just that! The mysteries of browser logic.

**pixeljam.com** uses this image enlargement hack combined with tiny abstract animated gifs to create a quick-loading, full-screen light show (**Figure 07.16**). The gifs themselves are only 6×6 pixels large, and less than 2K. They download unbelievably fast, and yet they still fill the entire screen with fast, colorful motion. The only problem is, if your processor is slow, your browser is likely to choke on the combined task of animating and enlarging such tiny gifs (in this case, you'll either see something that looks like a graphical malfunction, or you'll see nothing at all).

This image-enlargement technique combined with CSS layers is particularly useful because it lets you stretch a relatively small "virtual" background image so that it fills the entire browser window without tiling. You are still free to call in other images on top of this enlarged background using CSS layers.

## *onmouseover* **Functions**

Often, innovation comes from simply using a novel combination of ordinary techniques. Animated gifs and JavaScript image rollovers aren't particularly innovative. But when you combine the two, a mouseover suddenly causes a still image to burst into motion—or, conversely, a mouseover suddenly causes a moving image to freeze.

Actually, the **onmouseover** event can trigger any number of actions. Mousing over an image can cause an entire page's background to change if you simply program the mouseover event to toggle the visible/invisible attribute of a CSS layer. Or mousing over a link can forward the surfer to the next page quicker than he can say "Wuzza?"

Surfers are massively conditioned to think of clicking as the main action event. What better way to confuse them than by using mouseovers as the main action event? As Joe Surfer innocently moves his cursors across your web page, he might find himself unwittingly triggering pop-up windows, audio loops, and whatever other actions you decide to tie into the **onmouseover** event.

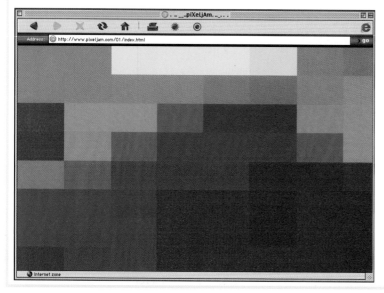

**Figure 07.16**

*pixeljam.com*

# Big Old Ugly HTML Text

Pixelated punk rock sites use big old ugly HTML text. What else is there to say? **<H1>**, **<H2>**, **<H3>**… Knock yourself out.

It should be obvious by now that pixelated punk rock is a usability expert's worst nightmare. These sites give their visitors a false sense of control, all the while manipulating and coercing them at every turn. But wait a minute! Haven't I just described most modern advertising in a nutshell?

In a sense, isn't the goal of advertising to cause people to purchase things they don't yet want? Don't advertisers seek to make consumers feel in control of the decision-making process, all the while manipulating them into exchanging their money for something they would not have otherwise purchased? (I realize I'm stepping on some toes here, but this *is* the punk rock chapter, after all!)

Should user empowerment and usability be the goal of an e-commerce web site? Do you really want to encourage surfers to wander around your online stores willy-nilly, reading this FCC-mandated earnings disclosure and that unmoderated product review? Instead, don't you want to funnel them as quickly as possible to that bright, candy-like "order now" button? Alrighty then!

Pixelated punk rock is just the psychedelic, hard-sell version of all e-commerce. It is e-commerce at its most bald-faced and unapologetic. Of course, the pixelated punk rockers aren't selling a product. They're selling a face-slapping paradigm shift (**Figure 07.17**). Order yours today while supplies last.

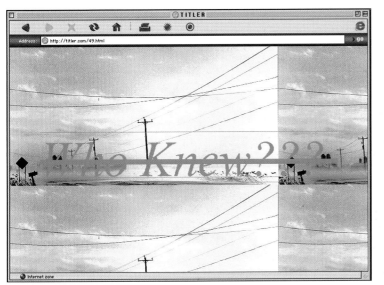

Figure 07.17

*titler.com*

119

# Sites Mentioned in This Chapter

http://www.titler.com

http://www.day-dream.com

http://www.dream7.com

http://www.requiemforadream.com

http://www.hi-res.net

http://www.soulbath.com

http://www.e13.com

http://www.pixeljam.com

"A sprite is a high-resolution programmable object that can be made into just about any shape—through BASIC commands... Using sprites requires knowing some more details about how the Commodore 64 operates and how numbers are handled within the computer. It's not as difficult as it sounds, though. Just follow the examples and you'll be making your own sprites do amazing things in no time."

—1983 Commodore 64 User's Guide, Section 6.1

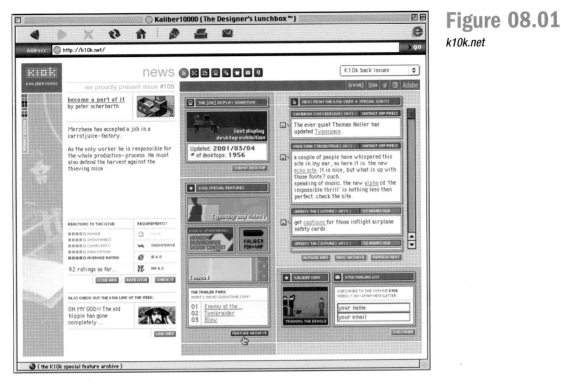

**Figure 08.01**

*k10k.net*

Back in the infancy of home computing, monitors could display only a limited number of colors and pixels. Creating screen graphics for these monitors was no small chore. High-resolution jpegs were out of the question. If you wanted to draw a person, you had to draw him one pixel at a time, using a very limited color palette. Today's desktop icon designers face a similar challenge. Although today's monitors can now display more colors, the standard desktop icon (such as a folder icon) can still be only 32×32 pixels large. Nevertheless, some amazingly detailed desktop icons have been created over the years.

Enter the web, with its limited bandwidth and variable screen resolutions. Sure, your high-resolution 250K jpeg collage looks brilliant on your million-color 21-inch monitor over your company's T1 line. But what about the poor schmo in Palookaville trying to access your site on his 14-inch 256-color

monitor over his 33K modem? SuperTiny SimCity Style to the rescue!

An entire generation of pixel Picassos have turned their talent to web design, with playful, impressive, and fast-loading results (**Figure 08.01**). Years of practice packing tons of visual information into tiny spaces have prepared these SuperTiny SimCity designers to overcome the web's limited browser window space and bandwidth. Who knew that the low-res video game designers of the '80s would be the darlings of the modern web design underground?

SuperTiny SimCity design is characterized first and foremost by the presence of tiny pixelated people, buildings, and objects. It is also known for its regular use of tiny pixelated fonts and its intense compartmentalization. As with other design styles in this book, SuperTiny SimCity can be applied 100%, or more sparingly. Either way, it has a charming, personable effect.

# Case Studies

Obviously, a style derived from video games is appropriate for fun, teen-oriented sites. What you might be surprised to discover is that this style is also used at **cnn.com**. Other than CNN, I'll look at a community site for graphic designers, a community site for desktop icon designers (duh), and a couple of personal sites. SuperTiny SimCity seems a natural style for a map site or a city directory site. Actually, any site with a lot of information that needs to be displayed in a relatively small space is a candidate for SuperTiny SimCity design (provided that the site can tolerate a bit of light-heartedness).

# Kaliber 10000: God Is in the Details

It wasn't the first to sport this style, but **k10k.net** gets credit for pushing SuperTiny SimCity web design past the novelty phase (**Figure 08.01**). K10K is a heavily-trafficked, content-intensive, regularly updated site with a robust, database-driven back end. And yet it maintains a friendly, approachable demeanor via its SuperTiny SimCity front end.

Almost every link on the K10K front page is an animated rollover. Particularly clever are the icon squares in the top menu that link to the site's main sections. Mousing over one of the squares morphs it into a circle, causing its icon to spin and descriptive text about that section to appear (**Figure 08.02**). Notice that these icons are relative to the size of your cursor pointer, so mousing over them "feels" as if you've actually touched something. The logo in the top-left corner loads first as a tiny animation that randomly changes every time you visit the site. So while you're waiting for the rest of the page to load (which still takes only a few seconds on a 56K modem), you've got something engaging to watch.

The "Kaliber Kam" in the bottom-right corner loads a random animation from the site's designers about their daily lives (at the gym, sleeping, brushing teeth, partying). Fortunately, you are spared a bandwidth-hogging webcam stream. Instead, these events are represented by pixelated animated gifs. All the gifs are cleverly constructed to include minimal amounts of movement over time, so they don't distract from the rest of the page's content.

**Figure 08.02**

*k10k menu*

"Lovingly crafted" is the best way to describe K10K. The closer you look, the more anal-retentive attention to detail you're likely to find. The entire site feels as if has been built by hand, one pixel at a time. And indeed, that's not far from the truth. From Per's custom back-end programming wizardry to Toke Nygard and Michael Schmidt's planning, coding, and graphics, K10K is the result of three focused, compulsive perfectionists who set out to deliver an impeccable user experience.

Note the amount of content on a page that's only 800 pixels wide. I count four columns and 14 discrete content sections. And yet the design actually feels spacious. This effect is achieved by some clever compartmentalization hacks and by the use of SuperTiny pixelated fonts. (I'll examine both techniques more closely in the aptly named "Techniques" section later in this chapter.)

# flipflopflyin: It's the Idea That Counts

**flipflopflyin.com** is the charming personal home page of one Craig Robinson. Craig is the originator of mini-pops, a gallery of miniscule pixelated caricatures of various celebrities (**Figure 08.03**). He excels at using the minimum number of pixels to convey the maximum amount of information.

Particularly clever is "Fun Fun Fun," a series of 10 animated scenes depicting various ways to have fun. Although each scene fills the whole screen, only a fraction of each scene is actually animated. The animations incorporate lengthy but meaningful pauses to convey narrative information—pauses that add nothing to the file size of the actual gif. A package recipient pauses before deciding to give the UPS man a hug (**Figure 08.04**). A Polaroid photographer pauses while waiting for his picture to develop. When the pixelated characters do move, it might only be to lift a cigarette or swing a golf club. This microcosmic approach actually increases visitor interest and suspense. You read a caption that says "photocopy your head," and you can't help but look extra close to discover just what is actually going on (**Figure 08.05**).

**Figure 08.03**

*Mini-pops (the Beatles, Moby, Bob Marley)*

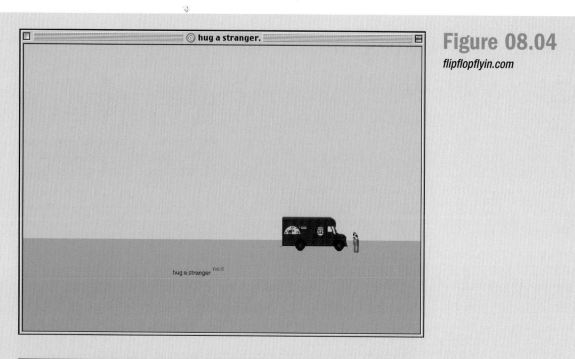

**Figure 08.04**

*flipflopflyin.com*

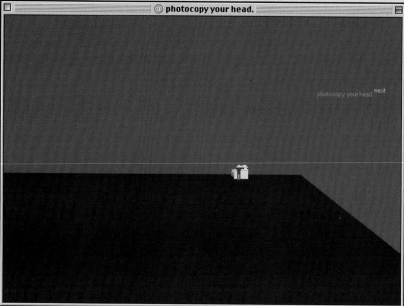

**Figure 08.05**

*flipflopflyin.com*

The "Fun Fun Fun" series is addictive because each scene is so novel (and so fast-loading) that you're bound to click through all of them just to see what's next. I've sat through many a 300K Flash animation in my day, but few have proven as riveting as these low-res animated gifs. If a picture is worth a thousand words, a clever concept ingeniously executed is worth a thousand pictures.

# db-db: In a Station of the Metro

Whereas K10K is SuperTiny SimCity Style sensibly applied, Francis Lam's **db-db.com** is SuperTiny SimCity Style full-on and cavorting wildly. db-db is still cleanly partitioned and fairly navigable, but you could hardly call it restrained. Its main Flash menu bar is a busily populated, animated subway station, with a train showing up at random intervals to let people on and off (**Figure 08.06**).

db-db is a personal experimental site. It is admittedly a bit extreme for most commercial interfaces. But I include it to make the point that the browser window need not look like a sheet of paper. Old-school game designers were very adept at creating pixelated worlds on 12-inch monitors. So why can't the browser window be thought of as a computer game screen rather than a sheet of paper? After all, the browser window is driven by software, and it uses light rather than ink to display information. When you start thinking about the web in terms of this alter-print paradigm, SuperTiny SimCity design starts seeming increasingly less oddball and more commercially legitimate.

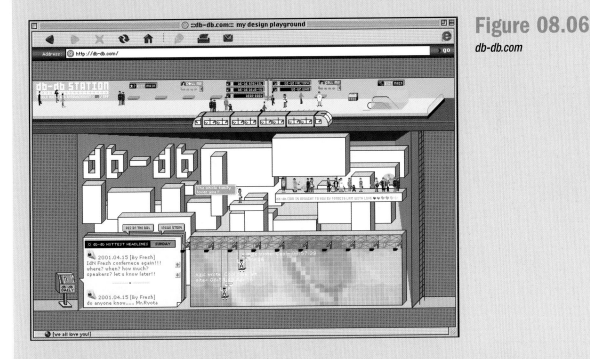

**Figure 08.06**
*db-db.com*

# cnn.com/CAREER: Will Work for Pixels

Lest you think SuperTiny SimCity is only for offbeat personal pages and designer community sites, the career section at cnn.com employs this style in both subtle and overt forms. It wouldn't make sense to have pixelated political figures on the front page of cnn.com, but pixelated coworkers and bosses are different. Employment is a very personal and often emotionally trying part of life, so Peter Rentz and the crew at CNN Interactive decided to lighten up CNN's career section with little pixelated worker guys.

On the regular career site, pixelated people are used as signature elements, but sparingly (**Figure 08.07**). The fonts on the regular site are not pixelated. There is partitioning, but not of the compact SuperTiny SimCity variety. CNN's regular career section is an excellent example of how pixelated characters can add an element of fun and lightheartedness to even the most austere and serious site.

## Figure 08.07

*cnn.com/CAREER*

For a more extreme example of commercial SuperTiny SimCity, you need only flash back to CNN's "Chaos in the Workplace" contest (**Figure 08.08**). Here, the SuperTiny SimCity vibe is ramped up considerably. Note the pixelated fonts in the header texts. Note the more tightly compartmentalized sections. The four pixelated gifs at the bottom of the page are even animated. What a fun way to present a contest that is, after all, supposed to be fun!

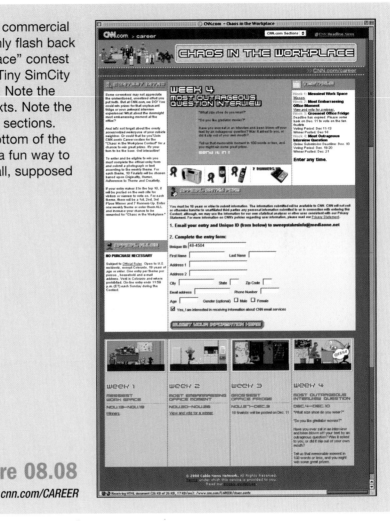

**Figure 08.08**

*cnn.com/CAREER*

# Techniques

Whereas the goal of the Gothic Organic Style is to be "real worldly," the goal of the SuperTiny SimCity Style is to be "simulated worldly." Surrender your longing for glossy photorealism. You are dealing with 8-bit gifs here, not jpegs. Luxurious anti-aliased cursive fonts are also out. You want to maintain your font edges, not lose them. Of course, there are hybrid sites where SuperTiny SimCity is used sparingly. Just make sure that whatever SuperTiny SimCity elements do appear on your site look "retro" enough to be at home in a pre-'90s video game.

# Tiny Pixelated People, Buildings, and Objects

Tiny pixelated characters and the worlds that surround them are the lifeblood of the SuperTiny SimCity Style. An excellent resource for learning how to make these pixel people is **iconfactory.com** (**Figure 08.09**). Icon Factory is a site that caters to the (predominantly Macintosh) icon-making community. This site holds a yearly "Pixelpalooza" icon design contest, and some of the works submitted are simply astonishing.

Making desktop icons is actually more complicated than merely making pixelated gifs for the web, but most of the same "drawing" techniques apply. Dave Brasgalla's "How To Make Icons" tutorial at Icon Factory tells you more than you ever wanted to know about bit depths, 3D shading, speculars, isometric grids, and Aaron Copland's relation to it all.

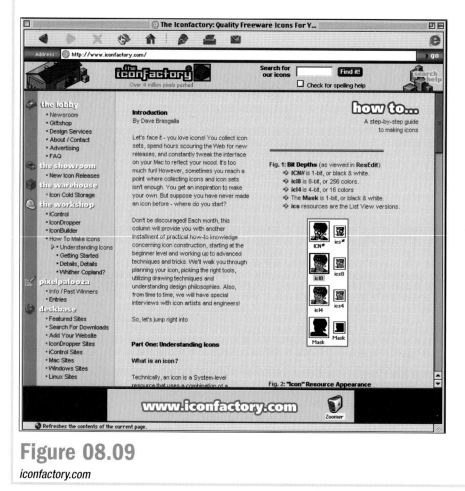

## Figure 08.09

*iconfactory.com*

Making your own pixelated world is not quite as easy as it might seem. Yet the tools and techniques themselves are very straightforward. Most master designers of the SuperTiny SimCity Style simply use the Photoshop pencil tool, set to a single-pixel brush size. If this approach sounds painstakingly tedious, it is. In the following brief interview, K10K's Toke Nygard shares some of his personal tips:

**Curt:** Do you just create your characters by hand a pixel at a time? Is there no shortcut?

**Toke:** No shortcuts. Just get going with the 1-pixel pencil brush in Photoshop. That is all there is to it.

**Curt:** Do you start off with a photograph and blur it? Do you reference a photograph? Do you reference a sketch?

**Toke:** For the figures, I might sometimes draw from a reference photo or straight from a model to get the clothing right.

For detailed background scenes, I might draw on top of a minimized picture.

**Curt:** When did you start making pixel people?

**Toke:** I started doing them way back on my Amiga in Deluxe Paint.

Basically, there is no quick way to master this technique, and there are as many different approaches to making pixel worlds as there are pixel artists. Start by studying pixelated art at the sites you admire. Download some gifs, open them up in Photoshop, enlarge them four or five times, check out exactly what's going on, and then begin your own exhilarating process of trial and error. You might want to start out designing small, simple objects (such as pencils and folders). As soon as you've got a feel for the technique, move on to people, animals, and landscapes.

# Pixelated Fonts

Every tiny pixelated character deserves a tiny pixelated font. The intense compartmentalization of the SuperTiny SimCity Style often demands the use of small fonts, and anti-aliased fonts at small sizes tend toward illegibility. Hence the popular use of pixelated fonts among SuperTiny SimCity designers.

There's no real magic to using pixelated fonts. Just find some that you like, and use them. Just make sure that you turn off anti-aliasing in Photoshop; otherwise, the edges will be smooth, which defeats the purpose.

Lots of free pixelated fonts are available at various digital foundries on the web, and new ones are always being created. Here is a short list of some good pixelated font sources:

• http://www.dsg4.com/04/extra/bitmap/
• http://www.miniml.com
• http://www.hi-type.com
• http://www.superlooper.de

Another approach is to design your own "paint" fonts in Photoshop. Start off with someone else's font at a small size, turn anti-aliasing off, and then use the pencil and eraser tool (both set to 1 pixel) to modify the characters—adding or subtracting serifs, carving away portions of strokes, and so on. Or simply use the 1-pixel paintbrush tool to build your own pixelated fonts from scratch. Although such fonts aren't "real" fonts in the sense that they can't be used via a keyboard, these homemade fonts can still be used in your web design, saved from Photoshop as text gifs. Of course,

your site will probably also use HTML-generated fonts in addition to "gif fonts." Most SuperTiny SimCity sites use Verdana 9-pixel, implemented via the CSS font control method outlined in the "Techniques" section of Chapter 9. nine pixels is about as small as you can take this font without losing legibility.

Pixelated fonts used as gif headers tend to make HTML body text look less lame. Wired's site is a good example of this effect (**Figure 08.10**). If the Wired logo were some fancy anti-aliased serif, the gap between the logo and the body text would be embarrassing—kind of like if you went on a date with a supermodel (assuming *you're* not a supermodel). But because Wired's logo is already pixelated, it sort of bridges the gap between plain HTML fonts and more-elaborate gif fonts—kind of like if you went on a date with someone who was more attractive than you, but not by much. The value of the HTML fonts is increased by association.

**Figure 08.10**

*wired.com*

# Extreme Compartmentalization

Few sites do the extreme compartmentalization thing better than K10K. Its orderly background partitions and tight 3D border edges obviously contribute to the site's compartmentalized feel. But K10K's back-end architecture also plays a crucial role in its hyper-efficient utilization of screen space. Not every front page link leads to a new second-level page. Some links simply swap out content areas right there on the front page.

For instance, clicking the feature archive link causes the "issue" content area to be replaced by the "special feature archive," while the rest of the front page remains unchanged (**Figures 08.01** and **08.11**). Clicking a link on the "other special features" submenu further invokes full descriptions and screenshots of whichever "feature" you've chosen (**Figure 08.12**). Only when you are absolutely sure which special feature you want are you transported out of the front-page environment and on to a new second-level page.

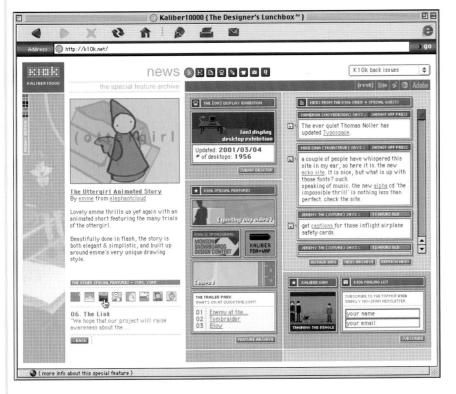

## Figure 08.11

*k10k.net*

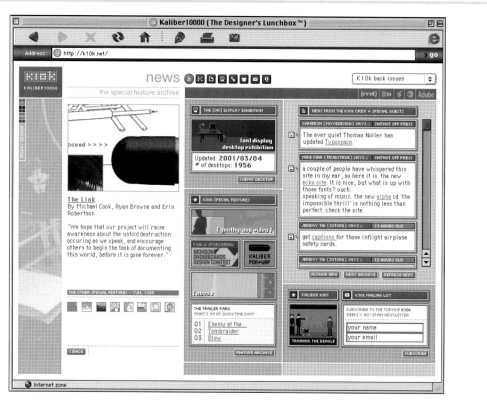

## Figure 08.12

*k10k.net*

This approach is ingenious. If I decide that none of the "special features" interest me, I don't have to back out of a second-level section to get back to the front page. I can comparatively evaluate all my options right there on the front page.

This feat can be accomplished through a combination of JavaScript and CSS layers. Create a number of different layers, and position them all in the exact same place on your page. Set one of the layers to **visibility: visible** and the rest of the layers to **visibility: hidden**. Then, when the user clicks the appropriate link, use the JavaScript **onclick** event to toggle the visibility of the affected layers. Have your JavaScript function set the initially visible layer to **visibility: hidden** and the newly selected layer to **visibility: visible**, effectively "swapping out" the two layers on your page. This added functionality takes a bit of extra coding, but the benefits gained in terms of usability are well worth the effort.

At first glance, SuperTiny SimCity design seems like a mere novelty, and indeed it *is* novel. But that doesn't keep it from being the right solution for certain sites. If you can convince your visitors to buy into the visual metaphor, there are actually many architectural and design advantages to this "video game screen" paradigm. And K10K alone proves that SuperTiny SimCity isn't just for kids anymore. What other site has won the prestigious High Five design award *and* has made it to the finals in the San Francisco Museum of Modern Art's Webby Awards? Millions of pixel-loving visitors can't be wrong.

# Sites Mentioned in This Chapter

**http://www.k10k.net**

**http://www.flipflopflyin.com**

**http://www.db-db.com**

**http://www.cnn.com/CAREER/**

**http://www.iconfactory.com**

**http://www.dsg4.com/04/extra/bitmap/**

**http://www.miniml.com**

**http://www.hi-type.com**

**http://www.superlooper.de**

**http://www.wired.com**

"To see a World as
a Grain of sand
And a Heaven in a
Wild Flower,
Hold Infinity in the
palm of your hand
And Eternity in an hour."

—William Blake

In the beginning was the word. Before there was Flash, before there was RealAudio, before there were gifs and jpgs, there was text. Plain HTML text. Early text-based browsers such as Lynx weren't too concerned with elegant typesetting, because the web had just been created to serve a loose collection of physicists exchanging research papers.

With the introduction of the **<font>** tag and its **face** attribute, web designers were finally able to break free from the browser's default fonts (predominantly Times and Courier). Furthermore, the **<font>** tag's **size** attribute gave designers more control over their font sizes than ever before. Although the **<font>** tag was a great improvement over the **<h1>**, **<h2>** series of tags, it still left much to be desired. HTML font sizes still varied noticeably from operating system to operating system. And if you wanted to modify your site's basefont size, you had to modify that piece of code on every single page of your site.

Finally, with the introduction of Cascading Style Sheets (CSS), designers can now control their font sizes down to the pixel. With CSS, even leading (controlling the amount of space between lines of text) is possible.

This type of cross-platform, cross-browser font control has ushered in a new wave of HTML purists. Inspired in part by the usability dictates of Jakob Nielsen, with his speedy download mantras and his least-common-denominator design approach, these new HTMinimaLists are proceeding to make beauty from code and very little else.

HTMinimaLists use their design skills to transform "simple" from boring to bold. And as always, the goal is effective communication—clear and uncluttered.

The 5k design competition (**http://www.the5k.org**) is a sort of HTMinimaList design Olympics. No entry site can be more than 5K. All but the most rudimentary pixelated gifs are out of the question. Patterns, movement, shapes, and interactivity must all be achieved via the hodgepodge of HTML, CSS, and JavaScript known as dynamic HTML. The 5k design competition is held in the spirit of the early MIT hacker wars—the person who can solve the problem with the least amount of code wins.

5k's winners astound by the force of their sheer ingenuity. One of my favorite pieces is Alex Barber's "The World's Smallest Art Museum" (**Figure 09.01**), which features a mini-Mondrian, a mini-Albers, and a mini-Rothko, all generated by pure code. Comic strip guru Scott McCloud observes, "The mastery of any medium using minimal elements has long been considered a noble aspiration." The 5k design competition takes that assertion to some freaky extremes.

Fortunately, you will never be asked to design a sub-5K site for a client. Nevertheless, of the 10 styles covered in this book, HTMinimaLism seems the most applicable to the majority of commercial web projects. With its clean, uncluttered look, its quick-loading gifs, and its no-nonsense attitude, this style is perfect for the company that wants to convey, "We mean business."

Ironically, there are currently few corporate
examples of HTMinimaLism in its pure form.
Why companies and design firms aren't
flocking to this style in droves is a mystery.
Perhaps companies want to feel they've
gotten their money's worth. If something
isn't beeping or whirling or swooshing,
they feel shortchanged. Whatever the case,
HTMinimaLism is a good style to mix with
almost any other style, simply because
fast download times and readable text can't
be bad.

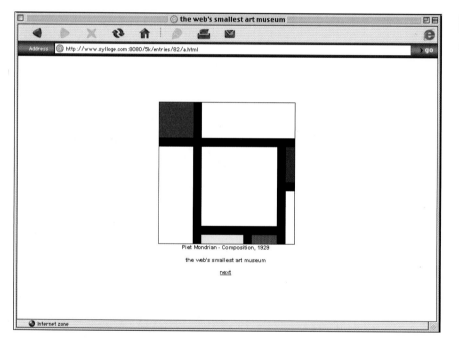

**Figure 09.01**

*the5k.org*

# Case Studies

HTMimimaLism is the right choice for any site that has large areas of plain text. This includes online newspapers, journals, trade publications, tutorials, and so on. It's also the perfect choice for e-commerce sites, or any "catalog" site that wants to display a large database of products.

# Simple for Sale: 37signals

The masters par excellence of HTMinimaLism are the Chicago designers of 37signals. Their site reads like a manifesto of the HTMinimaList Style (**Figure 09.02**). **37signals.com** does contain a rather extensive portfolio, but instead of focusing on the company's past achievements, the site focuses on a boldly opinionated set of "signals," 37 koans of wisdom that define the firm's design approach. For instance, here's an excerpt from Signal 25:

> *Just Because You Can, Doesn't mean you should.*
>
> *Sure, there are times when light type on a dark background is appropriate, but we don't think "it just looks cool" is reason enough.*
>
> *37signals believes that "hip" and "legible" don't have to be mutually exclusive. We love "cool" as much as the next person, but we also realize that part of our job is to make people's lives easier, not harder.*

37signals.com is HTMinimaLism in its purest form. Notice the abundance of white space, not just on the core page, but throughout the entire site. The core page has 46 links (about as many as **amazon.com** has "above the fold"). That's a lot of links, and yet 37signals.com is not cluttered. The only gif is the tiny logo in the top-right corner, weighing in at an anorexic 396 bytes. The colored dots throughout the site are not gifs. They are actually HTML bullets (**&#149;**) tweaked via CSS. The fattest image on the entire site is only 6.6K.

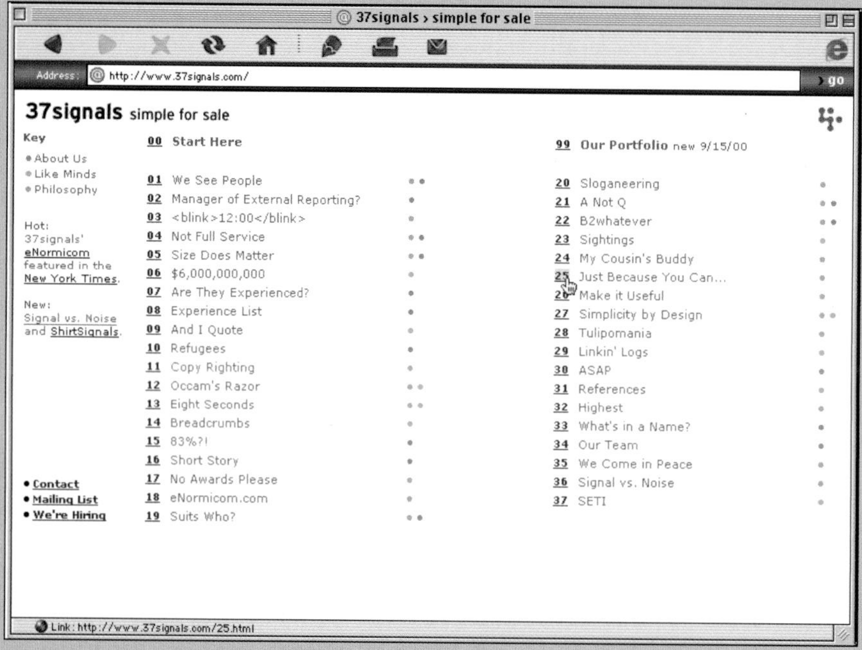

**Figure 09.02**
37signals.com

The core page looks as good at 800×600 as it does at 1000×800. It even looks good at 640×480. All of this is due to liquid table design, which allows the page to resize as needed without wrecking the layout. The HTMinimaList thinks of his web page not as a static magazine page, but as a fluid entity that morphs to accommodate the limitations and preferences of its viewer. The trick is to structure your pages so that they look good regardless of the user's operating system, screen size, number of available colors, and so on. Note that your pages don't have to look *the same* in all these different environments. (They won't. They can't.) They just have to look *good*. For an insightful explanation of the liquid design philosophy, read John Allsopp's "A Dao of Web Design" at **http://www.alistapart.com/stories/dao.**

The second-level pages at 37signals (**Figure 09.03**) are as impressive as the site's core page. Still uncluttered, they nevertheless present the visitor with four distinct ways to explore the site:

- You can click the HOME option in the bottom menu to return to the core page and surf from there.

- You're given a pull-down link menu of all 37 signals, with brief descriptions of each.

- You're given the numbers 1 through 37 in the bottom menu in case you want to hop straight to a specific signal. This long series of plain HTML numbers adds an intriguing visual element and reinforces the concept of the site.

- Most useful, you are given forward and back arrows in the bottom menu, facilitating an easy sequential perusal of the signals, which is probably the way most people wind up surfing the site on their first visit.

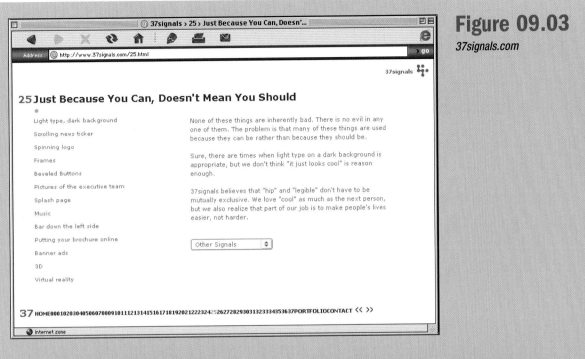

**Figure 09.03**
*37signals.com*

The bottom menu provides the added function of graying out visited links so that you can tell where you've already been. This is especially helpful when you're just hopping around.

All in all, 37signals is compelling, humorous, straightforward, helpful, and fast-loading. Its design is as refreshing as the prose of the signals themselves. A prospective client should come away from 37signals.com thinking, "These guys really know their stuff." And that, of course, is the site's purpose.

37signals proves that usability need not be ugly. Their site is an aesthetic treat, particularly in comparison to the generic undesign of Jakob Nielsen's **useit.com (Figure 09.04)**. Nielsen marginally achieves his safe goal of designing in a way that doesn't draw attention away from his content. Contrarily, 37signals surpasses its more ambitious goal of designing in a way that overtly enhances its content.

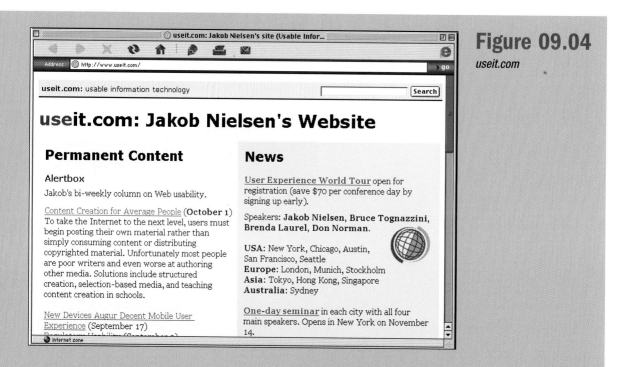

**Figure 09.04**

*useit.com*

# gettyone: Selling Made Simple

Sure, HTMinimaLism works well enough for a self-designed portfolio site, but what about a for-hire corporate site? With their efficient design of **gettyone.com** (a stock photography site), 37signals proves that HTMinimaLism can also succeed on a commercial site, particularly one with a large database of displayable products. gettyone is actually the perfect candidate for this type of minimalistic design. When you're selling actual images, do you really want your web site to be cluttered with a bunch of extraneous site-specific graphics competing with your product for attention? What if gettyone's logo had been a neon-blue light

bulb, looming large on every page of the site? Sure, it would complement a few featured stock images (by chance), but it would grossly clash with others. So the navigation and other site-specific elements at gettyone.com had to be low-key.

gettyone.com doesn't work at 640×480 (without having to scroll sideways), but it doesn't need to. The site's clients are graphic designers with large monitors. There is no liquid design here. The layout works at 800×600, and it simply recenters itself at anything larger, with little noticeable difference (**Figure 09.05**).

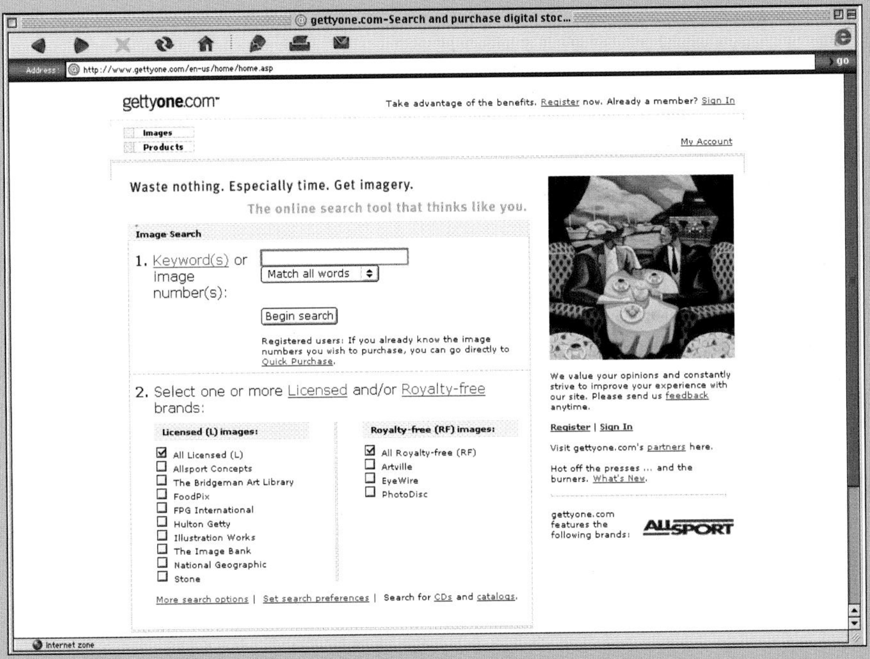

**Figure 09.05**
*gettyone.com*

Again, notice the abundance of white space. The core page contains 31 links, one search field, one pull-down menu, and 14 check-boxes. Yet it still has room to spare. 37signals chooses to devote most of the screen real estate to the search feature, because that's how most people will navigate the site. Yet gettyone.com doesn't feel like a search engine. Why?

Because, although the search feature is prominent, it's not dominant. The color image to the right balances the search section, not in size, but in emphasis. Right off the bat, you are given an example of the product. This featured image rotates, so every time you return you get a different core page image.

The core page has a header section, a left section, a right section, and a bottom menu section. And yes, these sections are partitioned by design elements. But notice how subtle the partitions are—mere dotted lines.

Only the search section is completely surrounded by lines. There are no ubiquitous tables with colored backgrounds. The only background color is white. Why doesn't amazon.com look this clean?

In all fairness, Amazon has a lot more stuff to sell. But gettyone could have prominently featured any number of bundled CD-ROM discount packets on the core page. They could have explained their membership options in detail. They could have talked about their copyright policy, or the resolution of their images, or any number of other things. But wisely, in the early information architecture stage of the design process, somebody had the wherewithal to realize that most people would be visiting gettyone.com for one reason—to search for and download images. With this primary purpose established, the core page could then be structured accordingly.

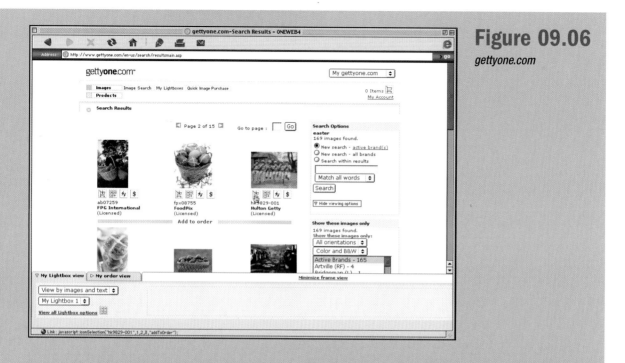

**Figure 09.06**

*gettyone.com*

When you perform a search at gettyone.com, even more features and options are added to the interface, but 37signals still manages to keep things uncluttered. They do this by continuing to use lots of white space and by giving information only as it's needed. For instance, there are four tiny, cryptic buttons beneath each image. Mouseover any button, and a clear explanation of that button's function appears (**Figure 09.06**). Mouseoff the button, and the explanation disappears. This is a sensible use of DHTML to present task-specific information only as needed.

DHTML is also used to reduce clutter via the use of a "Hide viewing options" toggle button. The operations menu on the right includes a myriad of configurability options, but if you click the "Hide viewing options" button, they all disappear (**Figures 09.07 and 09.08**). It is this type of compulsion to keep the interface clutter-free that makes HTMinimaLism appropriate for sites with lots of options and products.

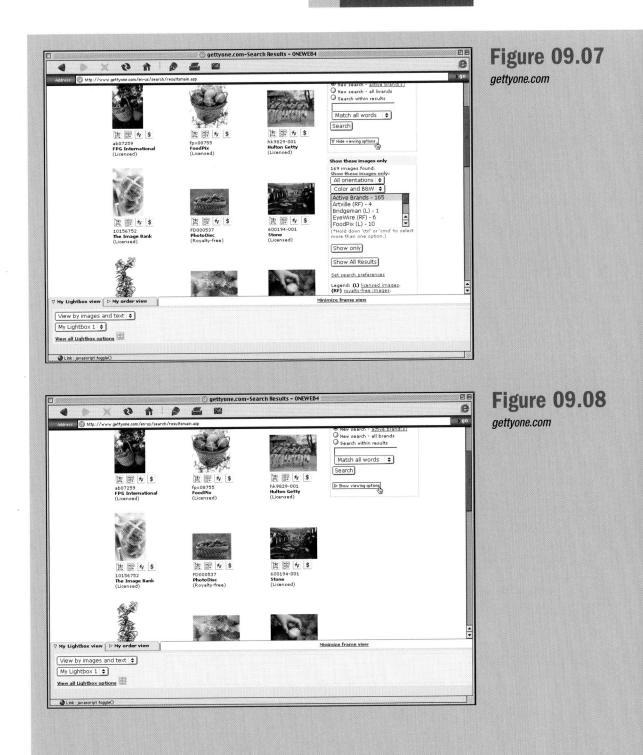

**Figure 09.07**

*gettyone.com*

**Figure 09.08**

*gettyone.com*

The brilliance of gettyone.com is in the details. For instance, the first time you visit the site, you're presented with a quick-loading splash page. On all subsequent visits to the site, you're taken straight to the core page. (This feat is accomplished by means of a small cookie.) The assumption is that the splash page must have positively influenced you on your first visit, or you wouldn't have come back. Now that you're back, there's no need to woo you repeatedly. You've got images to download.

Navigationally, 37signals uses space-saving pull-down menus aplenty at gettyone.com. They even deploy a couple of Amazonesque tabs here and there. But the navigation never diverts attention from the featured images themselves. Instead, this combination of sensible coding and minimalistic interface makes for a useful *and* enjoyable experience. Imagine that.

# A List Apart: Better Reading Through CSS

Jeffrey Zeldman's **alistapart.com** is best known for its useful and opinionated web design articles. But like all Zeldman-designed sites, A List Apart is built with an overt emphasis on readable web typography and a covert emphasis on fun (**Figure 09.09**). Note the abundance of eye-catching browser-safe colors and the strong area partitions. Note the outlined '50s-comic-book fonts and the bright, heavily-tweaked stock-photo montages. All these design elements are Jeffrey Zeldman trademarks. He crams a lot of color and character into a page whose fattest image is less than 12K.

Zeldman is an outspoken evangelist for Cascading Style Sheets and their ability to more legibly render browser-generated text. At alistapart.com, he practices what he preaches. Primarily using 11-pixel Verdana and judicious line leading, Zeldman's paragraphs are a pleasure to read (**Figure 09.10**). This type of CSS font rendering should be standard practice on any site with more than two paragraphs of text.

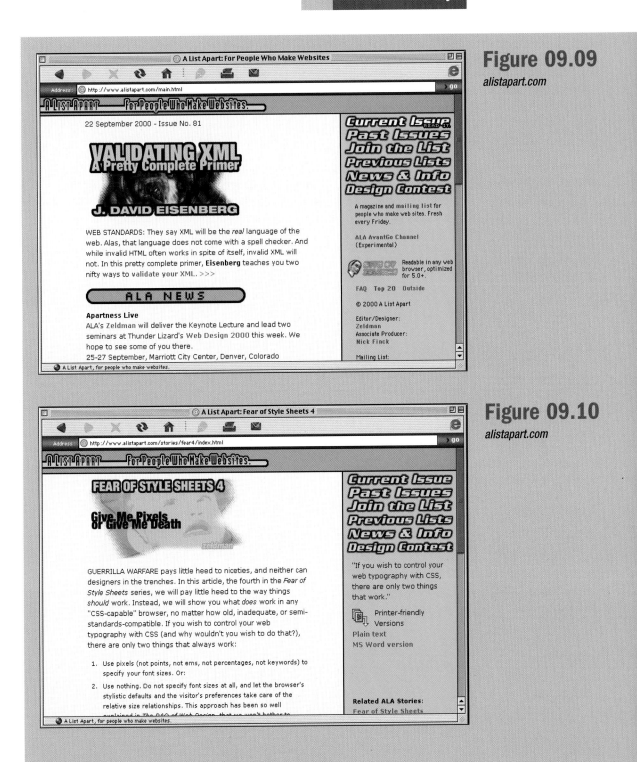

**Figure 09.09**

*alistapart.com*

**Figure 09.10**

*alistapart.com*

# endquote: Sometimes Nothing Is a Real Cool Hand

A bewildered admirer once asked Michelangelo, "How did you sculpt your famous statue of *David* from raw marble?" "Simple," Mike replied. "I just removed every part of the marble that wasn't David." I love that story, but I doubt it ever happened. Surely Michelangelo was too busy painting the Sistine Chapel to concoct such a pithy, anecdotal sound bite. The point of the story is: Great art is as much about what you leave out as it is about what you put in. The same could be said of great design.

This is why I'm a fan of **endquote.com** (**Figure 09.11**), the personal site of Seattle designer/programmer Josh Santangelo. Endquote looks as if Josh reckoned what he wanted to communicate, built a site that communicated it well enough, and then removed all the extraneous design elements until only the absolute essentials remained. Granted, endquote.com's core page is not the Sistine Chapel. But then, the Sistine Chapel isn't less than 10K, either.

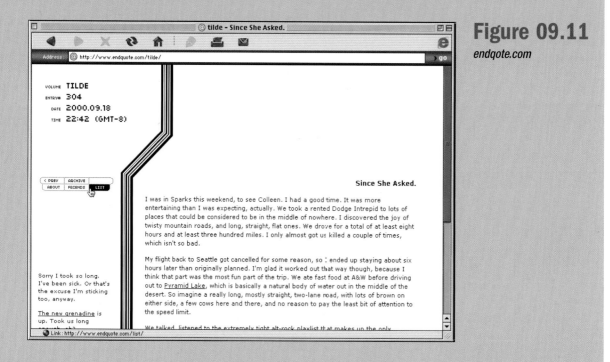

**Figure 09.11**

*endqote.com*

# Jovino: Relatively Speaking

In audio mixing, sometimes the best way to turn up a guitar solo is to turn every other instrument down. After all, loud is loud only in relation to what's not loud. The same is true of design. If every navigation button and swooshy logo screams "Check me out!" it's time to pick the element you want to be the loudest and turn everything else down.

jovino.com (**Figure 09.12**) is an excellent example of how a single, colorful, oversized element can "roar" when set in an otherwise "quiet" context. The classic commercial example of this technique is the much-discussed **apple.com** (**Figure 09.13**). Whether you like or dislike Apple's site, you will never accidentally overlook their featured special.

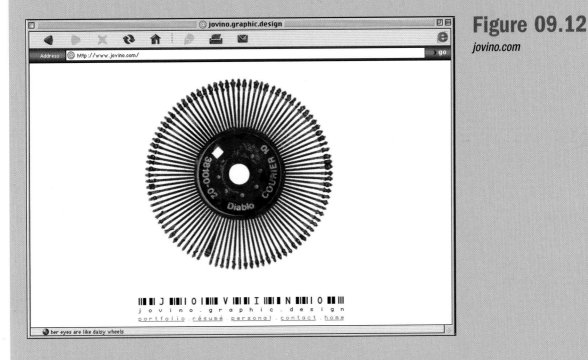

**Figure 09.12**

*jovino.com*

149

**Figure 09.13**
*apple.com*

# Techniques

The HTMinimaList designer eschews Flash and gaudy DHTML gimmicks. So what's left? First and foremost, HTMinimaLists focus on making HTML text look good. And the trick to good-looking HTML text is a decent understanding of fontography and color, coupled with your secret weapon—Cascading Style Sheets!

# CSS Font Control

Here is some good, safe, basic, cross-browser CSS code that will make your HTML text look better. There are as many ways to structure your style sheets as there are people with opinions. These are just my default preferences.

First, create a plain text document using the following text, and save it as styles.css:

```
b {font-weight: bold}

.large {font: 18px georgia, times, times new roman, serif}
.large A {text-decoration: none}
.large A:hover {text-decoration: underline}

.medium {font: 12px/18px verdana, geneva, helvetica, sans-serif}
.medium A {text-decoration: none}
.medium A:hover {text-decoration: underline}

.small {font: 9px/12px verdana, geneva, sans-serif}
.small A {text-decoration: none}
.small A:hover {text-decoration: underline}
```

Now create this HTML document:

```
<html>
<head>
<title>CSS font default example</title>
<LINK REL=STYLESHEET TYPE="text/css" HREF="styles.css">
</head>
<body>

<span class=large>
This Is 18px Georgia For Headers
</span>

<p>

<span class=medium>
This is the 12px Verdana for your main body text.<br>
And here's a line break to show the leading.<br>
And here's <a href="nowhere.html">a link</a>.
</span>

<p>

<span class=small>
This is the 9px Verdana for wee information.<br>
Again, a line break to show the leading.
</span>

</body>
</html>
```

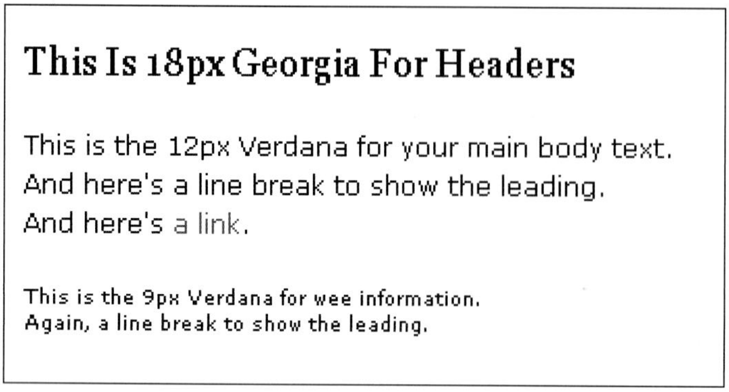

**This Is 18px Georgia For Headers**

This is the 12px Verdana for your main body text.
And here's a line break to show the leading.
And here's a link.

This is the 9px Verdana for wee information.
Again, a line break to show the leading.

## Figure 09.14
*CSS font examples*

Store both documents in the same directory, and your HTML page should look something like **Figure 09.14**.

Let's take a cursory look at how all this works. In the CSS document:

- **12px/18px** sets the font size to 12 pixels and the line leading to 18 pixels.
- The **A** and **A:hover** lines tell the browser, "Don't underline links until they are moused over." (**A:hover** is woefully unsupported in Netscape 4.)
- The fonts are listed in order of preference. If none of the specified fonts are available on the user's machine, his browser substitutes its own default fonts.

In the HTML document, the **<LINK REL=STYLESHEET TYPE="text/css" HREF="styles.css">** line must be present, or the styles will not be applied. The **<span>** tag is just a generic division tag that can be applied to any text. When your CSS **class** attribute is added, **<span>** modifies the text it surrounds accordingly.

Be warned that surrounding a table with **<span>** tags does *not* change the text within the table's data cells. To do that, you have to do one of the following:

- Put the modified **<span>** tags at the beginning and end of every block of text you want to modify, data cell by data cell (a pain).
- Specify **<td class="yourclass">** for the data cells that contain the text you want to modify (a bit more elegant).
- Define the **<td>** tag in your CSS document like so:

```
td {font: 12px/18px verdana, geneva, helvetica, sans-serif}
td A {text-decoration: none}
td A:hover {text-decoration: underline}
```

After you define **<td>** in your CSS document, all text contained within all table data cells is modified accordingly (without your having to add **class="myclass"** to anything).

For a more thorough study of CSS font control, check out Zeldman's "Fear of Style Sheets" series at **http://www.alistapart.com/stories/fear/index.html**.

# Color Schemes

What HTMinimaLism loses in the way of images it must make up in the way of code-generated color. Color is a crucial element of this design style, setting a site's emotional tone and giving meaning to key navigational elements. There is always the classic black-on-white scheme. 37signals.com uses a nice muted grey on white for its body copy text, with a near-black as the unvisited link color and a lighter grey as the visited link color (**Figure 09.02**):

```
<body bg=ffffff text=666666 link=333333 vlink=999999>
```

For a less-generic yet still conservative color scheme, **testpilotcollective.com** (**Figure 09.15**) sports a pleasant muted-blue palette:

```
<body bgcolor=6699CC text=ffffff link=ffffff vlink=FFFF00>
```

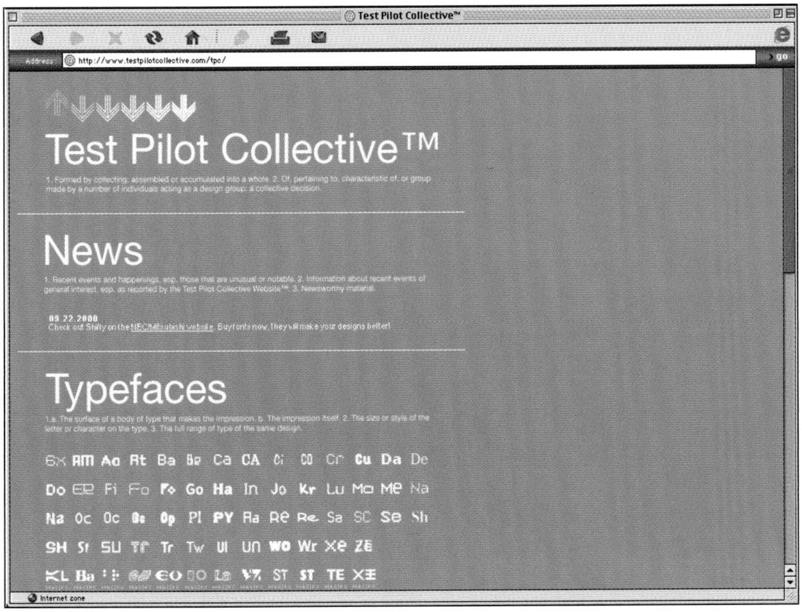

**Figure 09.15**

*testpilotcollective.com*

They use standard Helvetica rather than hip Verdana, and they control their text with the old-school **<font>** tags rather than Cascading Style Sheets. Consequently, their letters are larger on PCs than on Macs, but the difference is not really objectionable. Most of the uniqueness of Test Pilot Collective's core page is achieved via the use of their own custom-made fonts, served as thin loading transparent gifs and antialiased to match the page's background color.

These classy non-HTML fonts ennoble the otherwise plain HTML Helvetica. The blue background also has its own pseudo-anti-aliasing effect on the white HTML text. It's just an optical illusion caused by the relationship of these two colors on a monitor—and a happy accident it is. This color scheme is much less harsh than black on white, yet it is still reserved.

For an even more pronounced blue/off-white scheme, there's James Widegreen's **threeoh.com (Figure 09.16)**. Threeoh's palette is **<body bgcolor="328CC4" text="B7DDFD" link="7CDAFE" vlink="7CDAFE">**, applied to a miniscule 9-pixel Geneva. Because the colors are not browser-safe, Threeoh's text assumes a funky purple hue at 256 colors, but James doesn't care, because most of his visitors are graphic designers surfing on high-end systems.

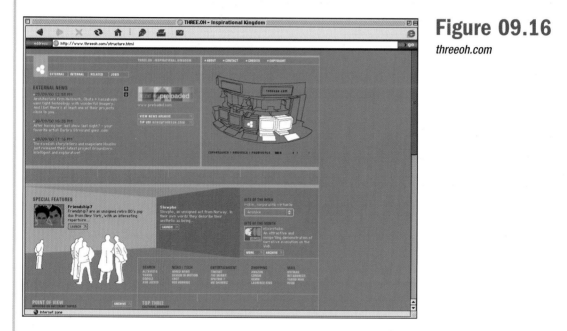

**Figure 09.16**

*threeoh.com*

Note the clever use of minimalistic gifs with strong outlines, all reinforcing the site's color scheme (and no gif is fatter than 7K). Threeoh's design approach is perfect for the web. Had these gifs been jpg photographs, the site would have taken much longer to load and would not have been as interesting or cohesive visually. Even the partition lines separating the page's various content areas reinforce the site's color scheme and its "outlined" approach.

Finally, on a darker note (literally), there's Joshua Davis's customized bulletin board, **dreamless.org**. Davis takes off-the-shelf BBS Perl software and customizes the front end to look... well, dark. The splash page sets the tone of the site (**Figure 09.17**)— just a straightforward message in a straightforward font.

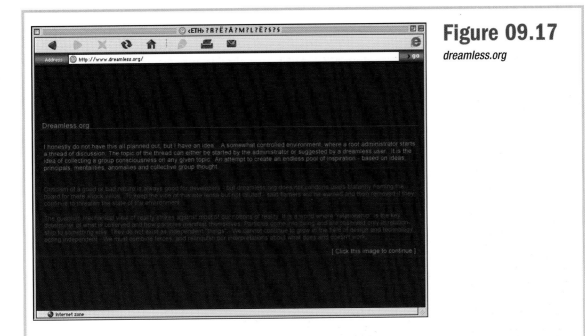

**Figure 09.17**

*dreamless.org*

dreamless.org's color scheme is completely grayscale: **<body bgcolor="#242424" text="#707070" link="#ECECEC" alink="#ECECEC" vlink="#ECECEC">** (**Figure 09.18**). The mouseover links are plain white. The tiny circular gifs that delineate unread posts are maroon, standing out like a sore thumb in this context (as intended). The font is plain old Arial. And that's it. Not exactly the optimum approach for **cartoonnetwork.com**, but very appropriate for Dreamless's target audience—young underground web site designers. Dreamless has a somber, back-alley feel that entices the type of person interested in debating the relative design merits of Marcel Duchamp while simultaneously repelling the type of person interested in discussing cute puppy names. The site's off-putting design acts as a kind of trial-by-fire rite of passage. If dreamless.org is too bleak and minimalistic for you, you probably won't enjoy the community.

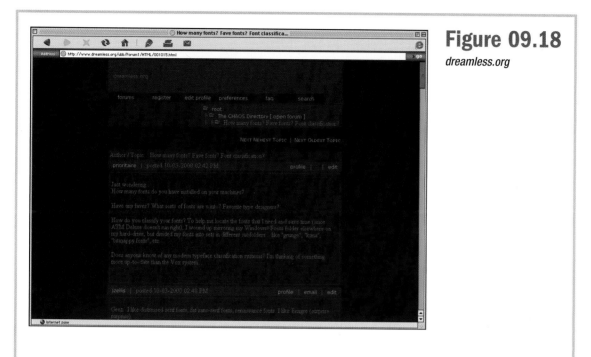

**Figure 09.18**

*dreamless.org*

Which color scheme is right for your particular project? That, of course, depends on the project. Dark text on a light background is the de facto standard. To achieve a more personal, inclusive feel, light text on a dark background sometimes works better. Whichever scheme you choose, be consistent about its application, and don't pick 50 different colors. This is ht*MINIMALISM*, remember?

# An Inflatable Alphabet

Back to Josh Santangelo's endquote.com to examine a little-used but ingenious gif alphabet hack. First, view the finished results (**Figure 09.19**). It might surprise you to know that each character is actually a miniscule 4×5-pixel gif. **Figure 09.20** shows the E gif up close. Each character is 3 pixels wide, with an extra pixel of blank space added to the right as a kerning mechanism to keep the characters from abutting each other.

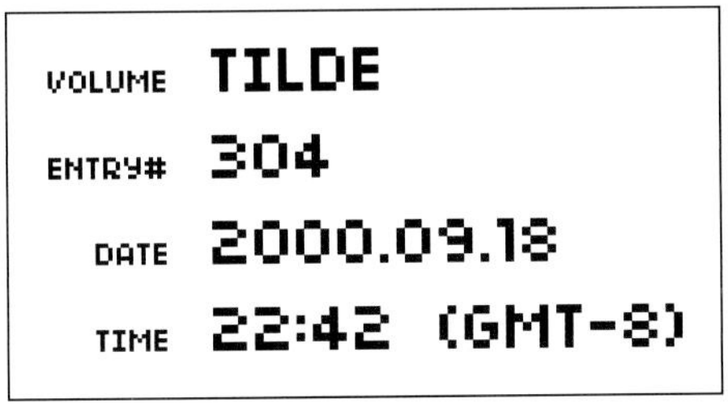

| VOLUME | TILDE |
| ENTRY# | 304 |
| DATE | 2000.09.18 |
| TIME | 22:42 (GMT-8) |

**Figure 09.19**

*endquote.com*

**E**

**Figure 09.20**

*A tiny E*

Here's the code that calls the first line of characters into the page:

```
<table border="0" cellpadding="0" cellspacing="10">
<tr>
<td align="right" valign="bottom"><img src="/images/letters/v.gif"
height="5" border="0"><img src="/images/letters/o.gif" height="5"
border="0"><img src="/images/letters/l.gif" height="5" border="0">
<img src="/images/letters/u.gif" height="5" border="0">
<img src="/images/letters/m.gif" height="5" border="0"><img src="/images/
letters/e.gif" height="5" border="0"></td>

<td><img src="/images/letters/t.gif" height="10" border="0"><img src="/images/
letters/i.gif" height="10" border="0"><img src="/images/letters/l.gif"
height="10" border="0"><img src="/images/letters/d.gif" height="10" border="0">
<img src="/images/letters/e.gif" height="10" border="0"></td>
</tr>
</table>
```

Notice that the small letters are called in at their actual height, while the big letters are called in at double their height. The browser acts as a makeshift font-enlargement device. This technique works because Josh's particular font is monospaced and aliased. A transparent spacer gif separates the words. After all the letters are loaded into the browser's cache, they don't have to be reloaded for the remainder of the session.

Realistically, the bytes saved by these miniscule gifs are more or less regained by the amount of HTML code it takes to call in and set the gifs. Still, this inflatable letter hack is a clever alternative to the same old HTML fonts. And if you're constantly changing your header text, inflatable letters might make more sense than re-creating a large multiletter gif every time you update your site. (Plus, you get to develop your own tiny pixelated fonts. Joy!)

# Table-Formed Fonts

Finally, an exercise in the absurd but possible. By day, Peter Rentz is the senior multimedia designer at CNN Interactive. By night, he invents fonts using HTML tables and a 1×1-pixel colored gif. When you get right down to it, web fonts are just a series of pixels arranged in a specific way. And HTML tables can arrange images in a specific way. Hmmm. What if you coded a series of table data cells that repeatedly called in the same single-pixel gif? And what if you arranged those data cells to form specific patters? And what if the patterns you formed looked like letters? You would have created the mesa.beta font (**Figure 09.21**).

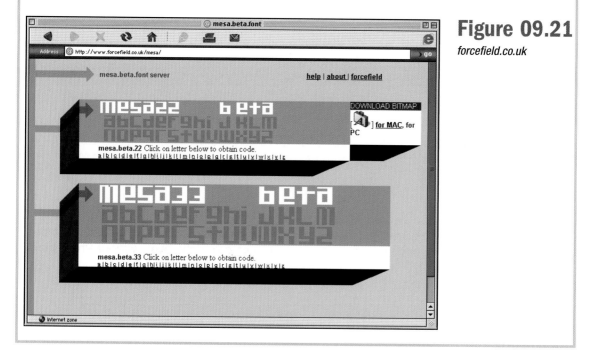

# Figure 09.21

*forcefield.co.uk*

To get an idea of how this works, here's the code that generates the 22-point letter K:

```
<!--start 22k-->
<table border="0" cellspacing="0" cellpadding="0">
        <tr>
                <td ><img src="pixel.gif" width="7" height="2" ></td>
                <td ></td>
                <td ><img src="pixel.gif" width="7" height="2" ></td>
        </tr>
        <tr>
                <td><img src="pixel.gif" width="7" height="8" ></td>
                <td></td>
                <td><img src="pixel.gif" width="7" height="8" ></td>
        </tr>
        <tr>
                <td><img src="pixel.gif" width="7" height="4" ></td>
                <td><img src="pixel.gif" width="7" height="4" ></td>
                <td align="left"><img src="pixel.gif" width="5" height="4" ></td>
        </tr>
        <tr>
                <td><img src="pixel.gif" width="7" height="4" ></td>
                <td></td>
                <td><img src="pixel.gif" width="7" height="4" ></td>
        </tr>
        <tr>
                <td><img src="pixel.gif" width="7" height="4" ></td>
                <td></td>
                <td><img src="pixel.gif" width="7" height="4" ></td>
        </tr>
        </table><!--end 22k-->
```

To obtain the mesa.beta font, simply visit **http://www.forcefield.co.uk/mesa/** and download the HTML. Create a colored 1×1-pixel gif, and you're ready to go. Granted, table-formed fonts aren't exactly the most direct way to generate web type. It would be much simpler to download Rentz's regular bitmapped version of the font, create your text in Photoshop, and save it as a gif.

But table-formed fonts are a crowning example of HTMinimaList ingenuity. With the advent of handheld net devices, solutions like table-formed fonts may yet come into their own as more than mere novelties. The point is, HTML is powerful in its own right, even without Photoshop, Illustrator, or Flash.

With more and more corporations subscribing to Nielsen's bare-bones usability approach, hopefully HTMinimaLism will come out of the closet and into its own. It is the logical style for any site that has large chunks of text or a large catalog of displayable goods (read: e-commerce).

New web designers tend to admire and emulate the flashier, graphic-intensive design styles, but I offer HTMinimaLism to you as a challenge and a thrill. Minimalistic design is rarely bland or boring. The satisfaction of creating usable, clean, scalable, and elegant sites out of nothing but HTML is its own reward. If nothing else, the promise of satisfied clients and site visitors is reason enough to pursue HTMinimaLism.

# Sites Mentioned in This Chapter

http://www.useit.com

http://www.the5k.org

http://www.37signals.com

http://www.alistapart.com/
stories/dao/

http://www.gettyone.com

http://www.alistapart.com

http://www.endquote.com

http://www.jovino.com

http://www.apple.com

http://www.alistapart.com/
stories/fear/index.html

http://www.testpilotcollective.com

http://www.threeoh.com

http://www.dreamless.org

http://www.forcefield.co.uk/mesa/

"Dave, I don't know how else to put this, but it just happens to be an unalterable fact that I am incapable of being wrong."

—HAL 9000 Computer

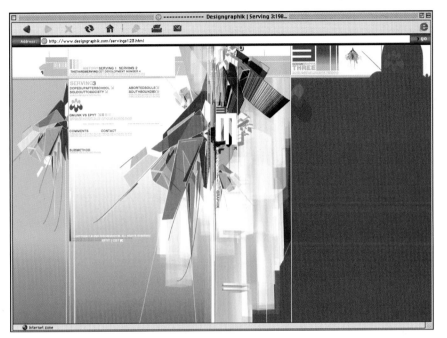

**Figure 10.01**

*designgraphik.com*

Probably the trendiest design style in the underground web design community right now is drafting table/transformer. In a community that's always striving for the next new look, using a $3,000 piece of 3D modeling software might seem like a pretty good way to keep people from ripping off your style. Alas, the proliferation of this style throughout the underground design community proves otherwise. Once pioneer designers like Mike Young showed the rest of the community what was possible using top-of-the-line modeling software, people began finding cheaper ways to achieve this sharding 3D look.

This chapter explores some 3D software solutions and techniques, but I'll spend most of the time examining some classic drafting

table/transformer sites. Just as owning Quark doesn't instantly make you a print designer, owning 3D modeling software doesn't instantly make you a drafting table/transformer designer. "It works if you work it," as they say. And nobody works this style like the few who pioneered it.

Drafting table/transformer sites usually have a bold conglomeration of sharding 3D shapes floating in seminegative space (**Figure 10.01**). These shapes are vaguely reminiscent of Transformer robot toys, giving the style its futuristic, sci-fi look. Officious-looking illegible text often accompanies these 3D shapes. Inspired by instruction manuals and small-print disclaimers, this miniscule text is for effect only and is not meant to be read.

Cryptic navigation elements are also a drafting table/transformer hallmark. Your navigation might be five tiny squares that must be moused over before they yield their destinations. Visiting a drafting table/transformer site feels kind of like thumbing through the interactive instruction manual for a futuristic interplanetary fighter craft. (Not that I've ever thumbed through such a manual. But I have seen *Blade Runner* several times.)

Although not overtly inspired by graffiti, these sharding shapes resemble some of the more radical 3D graf styles of the '90s. Furthermore, Zaha Hadid's experimental architecture looks eerily drafting table/transformerish. Whether these connections are accidental or intentional, drafting table/transformer definitely has a tight, progressive feel. Forget old-school, neo-techno bevels and chrome textures. Forget all those mid-'90s rave posters and Orbital CD covers. Drafting Table/Transformer Style is the "new" face of the imagined techno-future—at least for now.

# Case Studies

The Drafting Table/Transformer Style is commercially appropriate for any branding site that wants to associate its products with an advanced, intelligent, and hip future. Edgy and aggressive, drafting table/transformer has been used to promote flashy cars and angsty/mod teen music. It would be ideal for promoting a science fiction film or novel. I could even see it being used to build a leading-edge technology site (less the cryptic navigation). However, this style probably won't be cropping up at **marthastewart.com** anytime soon.

Before examining this style's more-subdued commercial applications, let's check out some personal sites where drafting table/transformer design has been unapologetically unleashed in all its sharding fury.

# Mike Young: The Ghost in the Machine

Of all the Jedi designers who sport this style, Mike Young stands out when it comes to crafting complex sharding vectors (**Figure 10.01**). Unlike most drafting table/transformer designers, who seek to be intimidating and fierce, Young's work is bright, colorful, and often humorous (**Figure 10.02**). Whereas most designers are still trying to figure out how to even pull off this style, Young is already exploiting its strengths and fusing it with other styles to make striking artistic statements (**Figure 10.03**). Much of Young's recent work is done in Flash, with tiny blipping and flitting machine-like animations adding to the style's overall futuristic effect.

Young's shapes always begin somewhere off the screen and flow into the open window space. This gives them a feeling of explosive motion, even though they aren't actually animated. The sharper the shards, the more aggressive the design's mood.

Mike Young's personal site, **designgraphik.com**, is navigationally cryptic—and intentionally so. Since most of its links lead to abstract gallery pieces, naming each link explicitly beforehand would detract from the site's exploratory nature. However, the links that *need* to be labeled (such as links to previous iterations of the site) are labeled clearly enough.

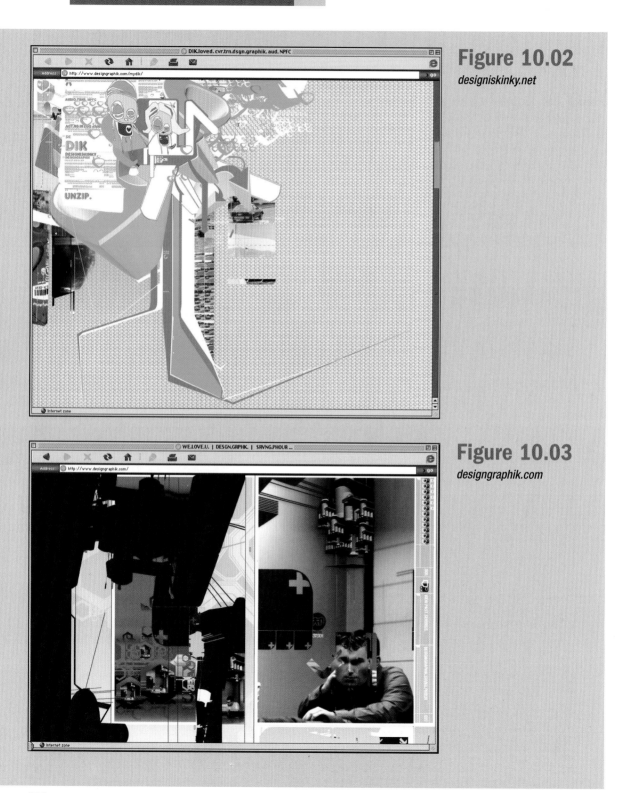

**Figure 10.02**
*designiskinky.net*

**Figure 10.03**
*designgraphik.com*

When Young does use words to identify links, he sets them in bold sans-serif all caps (**Figure 10.01**). Rolling over these text links sometimes changes the words themselves. For example, one prerollover link reads "SKIP THIS LOAD." Rolling over that link transforms those words into "I WISH YOU THE BEST OF LUCK ONLINE." This sort of "call and response" rollover navigation can be a pleasant surprise when used sensibly. And, of course, design-graphik incorporates the obligatory, illegible small print as abstract design—set in sans-serif all caps (as far as I can tell).

# chapter3: A Darker Shade of Pale

I mention Jens Karlsson's Desktop Imperium at chapter3 (**Figure 10.04**) because it is an excellent example of the Drafting Table/Transformer Style, but also to contrast it with Mike Young's work. Notice how Karlsson's harsher shapes and muted palette darken the mood of this site. Whereas Mike Young's shards seem benign and friendly, like octopi or seaweed, these shards seem dark and menacing, like aggressive enemy spaceships.

**Figure 10.04**

*chapter3.net*

# Hyperprism and MTV2 UK: Spatial Navigation

What would happen if you took these 3D shapes and incorporated them into your site navigation? Your sites might begin to resemble William Gibson's fictitious cyber-space, a 3D datascape of information as structure. Neither Hyperprism nor MTV2 comes anywhere close to Gibson's full-blown sci-fi vision, but they do provide a glimpse into what such a web might look like.

Hyperprism is simply a personal portfolio in the form of a Flash file (**Figure 10.05**). Click the DESIGN link, and a submenu emerges. Mouse over that submenu, and options appear. Click one of those options, and a pop-up window appears, containing the data you requested. Interactive Flash navigation is nothing new, but incorporating it into a sharding 3D landscape is.

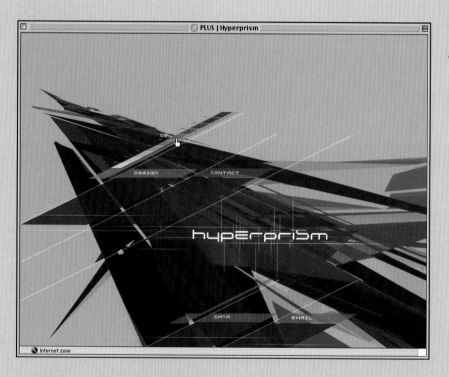

## Figure 10.05

*bmrc.berkeley.edu/plus*

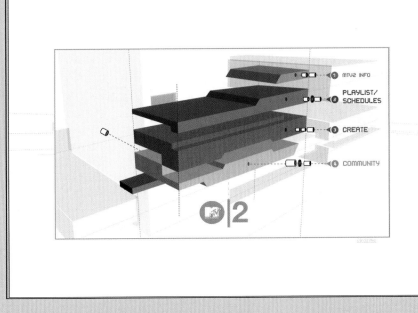

**Figure 10.06**
*mtv2.co.uk (level 1)*

MTV2's UK site takes this concept of spatial Flash navigation and turns it into what can only be described as a virtual city. At the core level of MTV2, you are given a choice of four floating planes, each mapped to a content section of the site (**Figure 10.06**).

Clicking the red CREATE plane causes it to shoot forward. You are then taken to a deeper level of the site, and to an entirely separate Flash file (**Figure 10.07**). But it doesn't feel like a new Flash file. Instead, it feels like you have "ridden" the red plane forward and are now hovering with it over some new part of the virtual city below.

At this second level, you are given four new options. Clicking ARTIST SEARCH causes the red plane to recede, and you are presented with a scrollable window and yet another set of menu options (**Figure 10.08**).

Although MTV2's design is admittedly slick, the real innovation here consists of mapping the navigation elements to physical "spaces" and presenting the site as a metaphorical "ride" through a floating city. You feel as if you are exploring a place rather than leafing through a database. This altered perception is all due to an intentional and well-executed illusory design narrative. MTV2 not only allows you to surf their site; they allow you to "star in" your own navigational "story."

Is this 3D city approach appropriate for Wall Street day traders trying to get stock prices at the drop of a hat? No. Is this 3D city approach appropriate for MTV kids interested in discovering when they're most likely to catch the new Moby video? Yes.

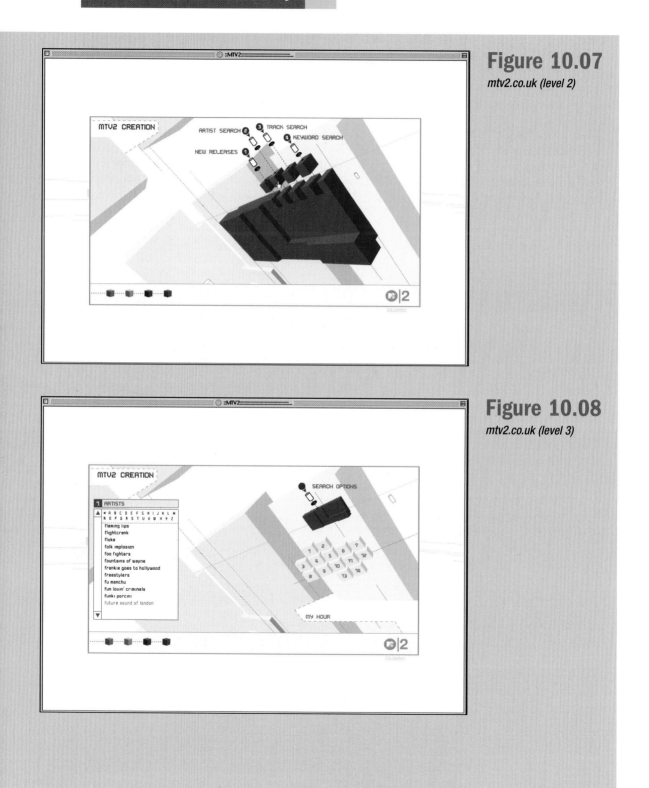

**Figure 10.07**
*mtv2.co.uk (level 2)*

**Figure 10.08**
*mtv2.co.uk (level 3)*

# Mercury Vehicles: Unbutton Your Soul

The Mercury Vehicles site uses drafting table/transformer Flash to target a 30-something "adventurous, yet thrifty" demographic (**Figure 10.09**). After a flourish of zipping arrows and flitting, illegible small print, the Mercury Cougar animation displays this catchy mantra: "Unbutton your soul." ("Unzip your wallet" might be more accurate.) At any rate, a major American automobile manufacturer is using drafting table/transformer to brand their cars online. The fonts are less extreme, and the 3D objects are less jagged, but the effect is still machinated, technical, and futuristic. Not surprisingly, these animations were created by Mike Young.

Note that only the animations are in Flash. The rest of the site's navigation and text are HTML-based. So not every drafting table/transformer site need embrace MTV2's all-or-nothing spatial navigation approach. If a Mercury Vehicles surfer doesn't feel like waiting for the Flash animation to download, he is free to move on. The rest of the site's navigation does not rely on Flash.

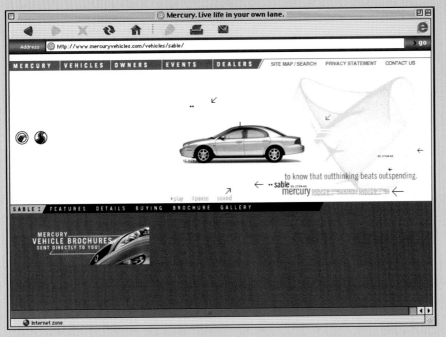

**Figure 10.09**

*mercuryvehicles.com*

# Techniques

Apart from the general "look and feel" observations already discussed, the specific "impartable" techniques of the Drafting Table/Transformer Style boil down to two elements—sharding shapes and illegible fonts.

# 3D Modeling Software

Just as "use Quark" is not really a print design technique, "use 3D modeling software" is not really a web design technique. The problem is, specific instructions vary wildly, depending on which 3D modeling software you choose. What I can do is introduce some popular 3D modeling software options and talk a little bit about each one.

Professionals like Mike Young use discreet's 3ds max or its newer iteration, 3ds max 4 (**http://www.discreet.com**). This solution can cost you around $3,000, and it's currently available only for Windows systems. 3ds max is the type of software that special-effects creators use, and it is more than sufficient to create even the most intricately rendered sharding vectors for the web. It supports tons of file formats and can even export vector images straight to Flash for subsequent animation. 3ds max is the Rolls Royce of 3D software options.

An infinitely cheaper 3D software alternative to 3ds max is Strata 3D, which is absolutely free (**http://www.3d.com**). True, the Strata 3D installer is a 20M web download, but you can also order it on CD-ROM for less than $40. If you've never experimented with 3D software, you might want to start with Strata 3D and work your way up.

Whichever 3D software you use, the idea is to create some shapes, render them from several angles, export them into Photoshop, layer them, add effects, and try to come up with something that looks cool and futuristic.

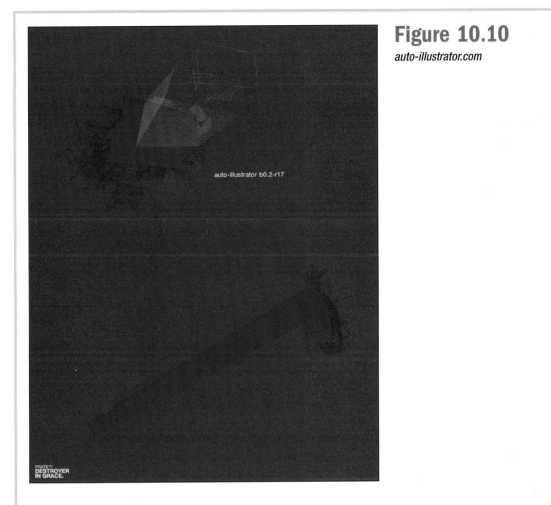

## Figure 10.10

*auto-illustrator.com*

Apart from pure 3D solutions, several 2D solutions work quite nicely. Adrian Ward's free auto-illustrator software is one such solution (**http://www.auto-illustrator.com**). It auto-generates 2D sharding shapes for you. Just keep cranking them out until you get some you like, and then call them into Illustrator or Photoshop for further tweaking (**Figure 10.10**).

Yet another sharding shape shortcut comes in the form of a plug-in. Kai's Power Tools Vector Effects 1.5 (**http://www.corel.com**) is a suite of Illustrator plug-ins, one of which is the aptly named "shatterbox"

plug-in. This plug-in creates a box around whatever shape you've made in Illustrator, and then (wonder of wonders) it shatters the box. You can adjust the number of shatters, the amount of displacement, and so on.

Finally, Mike Cina has developed an ingenious method for creating 3D wireframe shapes in Illustrator using the "blend" tool. His technique is revealed in this Adobe online tutorial: **http://www.pacific.adobe.com:80/web/ gallery/trueistrue/howto.html**.

# Tiny Illegible Type

Making tiny illegible type is not that hard. Here are a few things to avoid. Use an evenly spaced font—preferably a sans-serif. You don't want to use a cursive font or some wacky irregular font, because it will look zany and organic, and the idea here is to look machinated. Make sure your font is anti-aliased. Bitmapped fonts are too legible. Even at small sizes, people might actually be able to read them. Tiny anti-aliased fonts blend and artifact until the eye gives up making any sense of them. Finally, keep your font tracking at 0 or below. It's OK to have some space between the words, but there shouldn't be any space between the letters.

At this point, some usability expert somewhere is pulling his hair out at the sheer irony of a tutorial on how to make your text *illegible*. All I can say is, "Don't pull out all your hair yet. Save some for the last chapter."

With its aggressive/mechanical vibe, the Drafting Table/Transformer Style isn't for every site. But as the Mercury Vehicles site illustrates, this style in the right context can achieve striking and memorable results. 3D modeling is not for the faint of heart, but for those who have the patience and inclination, the Drafting Table/Transformer Style is a sure way to achieve a fashionable, futuristic look, all the while avoiding the chewy chunks of old-school, techno-chrome degradation.

# Sites Mentioned in This Chapter

http://www.designgraphik.com

http://www.designiskinky.net

http://www.chapter3.net

http://bmrc.berkeley.edu/plus/

http://www.mtv2.co.uk

http://www.mercuryvehicles.com

http://www.discreet.com

http://www.3d.com

http://www.auto-illustrator.com

http://www.corel.com

http://www.pacific.adobe.com:80/
web/gallery/trueistrue/howto.html

"Come with me
And you'll be
In a world of pure imagination.
Take a look
And you'll see
Into your imagination.

We'll begin
With a spin
Traveling in the world of my creation.
What we'll see
Will defy
Explanation."

—Willy Wonka

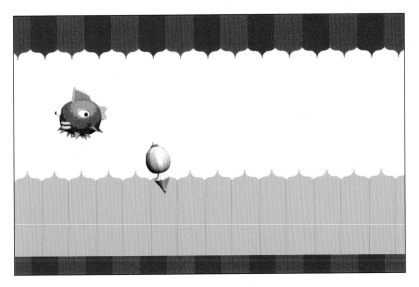

**Figure 11.01**

*futurefarmers.com*

If SuperTiny SimCity Style had a big sister, it would be 1950s Hello Kitty Style. 1950s Hello Kitty design is a funky amalgam of cuddly Japanese comics, Swiss marionettes, animated woodmation characters from those bizarre TV Christmas specials (remember Burl Ives as a wooden snowman and the elf who became a dentist?), and 1950s chrome metal campers. The style seems to have sprung fully formed like Athena from the mind of San Francisco designer and artist Amy Franceschini in the early days of the web (**Figure 11.01**). She has been expanding its parameters online and off ever since.

Franceschini's designs invariably involve animated 3D bubble people cavorting around some organically stylized, surrealistic environment. But there is more to 1950s Hello Kitty than bubble characters. The style is also known for its pastel palettes, its irregularly rounded borders, and its use

of retro-futuristic fonts. When I say "retro-futuristic," think drive-in theater signs, Las Vegas casino signs, and *The Jetsons*. Like every era, the '50s had its own particular version of what "the future" would look like. 1950s Hello Kitty designers draw inspiration from this retro-futuristic reservoir, even as they construct their own unique brand of contemporary kitsch.

I don't want to make too much of this fact, but an inordinate number of 1950s Hello Kitty designers are women—just as an inordinate number of drafting table/transformer designers are men. Not surprisingly, the two styles couldn't be more different. Drafting table/transformer leaps out and attacks you, whereas 1950s Hello Kitty lures you in. The one thing these two styles have in common is their use of 3D modeling software.

# Case Studies

You might have guessed that 1950s Hello Kitty design is perfect for a Power Puff Girls fan site, a teen girl community site, and a Hello Kitty theme park site. And you'd be right. But that's just the tip of the iceberg. In this section, we'll see this style applied to a greeting card site, a gardening site, a photographer's portfolio site, and an experimental e-zine. 1950s Hello Kitty design is probably a bit off-center for **usatoday.com**, but it might be just the approach for **yahoo.com** 2.0. Furthermore, Franceschini's client list includes Adobe, The *New York Times,* Lucasfilm, and *Wired* magazine—proving that this style is not just for the "Girls Rule/Guys Drool" demographic.

# Amy Franceschini: Welcome to My Daydream

Amy Franceschini is known in the art world and the design world for her peculiar creativity. Futurefarmers is her "flagship" site (**Figure 11.02**), which acts as a hub for her other online projects. From Futurefarmers, you can access **nutrishnia.org**, Franceschini's more experimental site (**Figure 11.03**); *Atlas* magazine, the progressive e-zine for which she designs (**Figure 11.04**); and numerous commercial examples of her print and new-media work.

The Futurefarmers motto is "Cultivating Your Consciousness," and it is apparent from the moment you visit the site that someone is out to shift your paradigm. The menu bars float around and don't sit still until you mouse over them. The core page features a bubble girl jumping on some sort of floating, lily-pad-like trampoline, which gives way slightly whenever she lands on it (**Figure 11.02**). Gravity is simulated, but in a slow-motion, "walking on the moon" type of way. This allows the bubble girl to do all sorts of fabulous backflips. Mousing over the Futurefarmers masthead reveals the company's contact information dramatically plastered across the page's entire background (**Figure 11.05**).

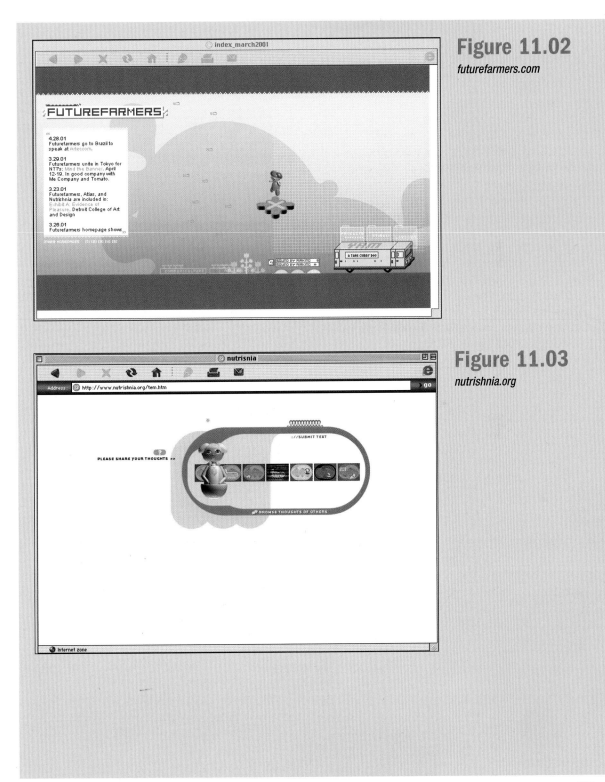

**Figure 11.02**

*futurefarmers.com*

**Figure 11.03**

*nutrishnia.org*

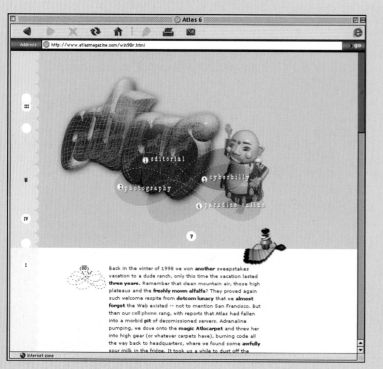

**Figure 11.04**

*atlasmagazine.com*

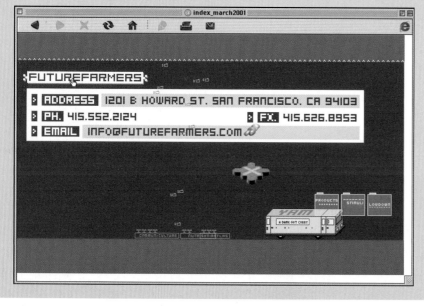

**Figure 11.05**

*futurefarmers.com*

Strange animated details like this (and hundreds more) gradually undermine your sense of stability, until you start feeling like you're not on a web site at all. Futurefarmers actually feels more like a video game than a web site, except that there is no real competition, and nobody ever loses. You just hang out.

Franceschini has been able to apply this same design style to more traditional projects while still maintaining her character-istic otherworldly mood. At *Atlas* magazine, for example, Flash animation is replaced by DHTML animation, but the objects still continue to move (**Figure 11.04**). The links in the menu bar on the left float up and down, and a flying-carpet rider zooms past at odd intervals. Even the static "atlas" graphic appears to be in motion because of its angle and 3D rendering.

Drilling down a couple of levels reveals some exquisite campiness. At level 2, you discover a mystical bull menu (**Figure 11.06**), followed at level 3 by your basic funky-chicken header menu (**Figure 11.07**). Atlas's menus and submenus, although unorthodox, are still fairly intuitive. The numbers under the chicken link to various photographs at the site's next level. The bull and the front-page "atlas" menu continue throughout the site as navigation elements, making it easy to jump straight to another section without having to use your browser's Back button. All this attention to hierarchical detail demonstrates that the 1950s Hello Kitty Style can succeed even at a content-intensive site.

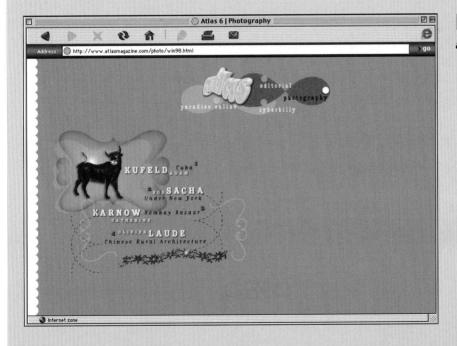

## Figure 11.06

*atlasmagazine.com (level 2)*

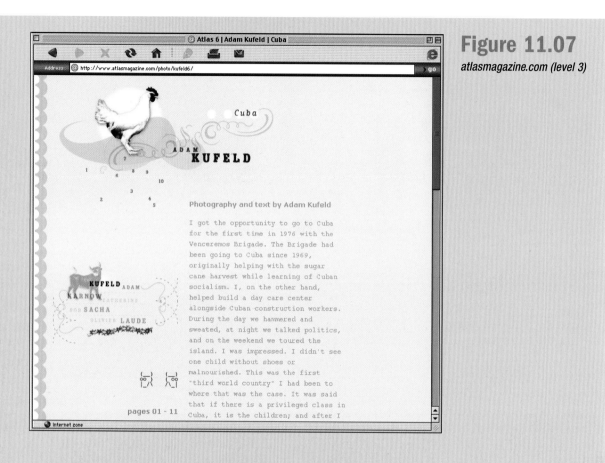

**Figure 11.07**
*atlasmagazine.com (level 3)*

Olivier Laude's online photography portfolio reveals an even more conservative application of 1950s Hello Kitty (**Figure 11.08**). The site still has all of Futurefarmers' characteristic baroque embellishments, but the curves, colors, and 3D effects are dialed back to focus our attention on the photographs themselves. The navigational interface is clean and intuitive, while still maintaining a touch of whimsy. **olivierlaude.com** is an excellent example of 1950s Hello Kitty design applied sparingly.

**Figure 11.08**

*olivierlaude.com*

# Post Tool: Exuberant Minimalism/Minimalistic Exuberance

Post Tool is another award-winning San Francisco design firm that specializes in 1950s Hello Kitty design (**Figure 11.09**). Their portfolio site features a gorgeously smooth, animated fabric ripple effect, rendered in Flash. Post Tool's layout is much more minimalistic than Futurefarmers', while still achieving that 1950s Hello Kitty vibe. Post Tool's navigation is ingenious in its straightforwardness. Click a link on the main menu, and you get a submenu to its immediate right. Click a link on the submenu, and the content appears to its immediate right (**Figure 11.10**). Note the uncluttered feel and the vast amount of white space on the page, proving that playful need not mean claustrophobic. These are *micro-cosmic* worlds, after all, with plenty of room to spare.

**Figure 11.09**
*posttool.com*

**Figure 11.10**
*posttool.com*

# Avant Card and You Grow Girl: Commerce with an Impish Grin

I hesitate to call either Avant Card or You Grow Girl "commerce." Avant Card has a unique business model involving a combination of government funding and private corporate subsidization. The bottom line is, their cards are made available for free throughout Australia. And their web site has a free e-cards feature as well.

To showcase the creativity of these unique cards, the design firm Toy Satellite chose to use a bright 1950s Hello Kitty layout for the Avant Card web site (**Figure 11.11**). Note the 3D '50s fonts, the pastel colors, and the rounded organic borders—all well-implemented characteristics of this style.

**Figure 11.11**

*avantcard.com.au*

You Grow Girl began as a personal project for gardening enthusiast and Fluffco web designer Gayla Sanders (**Figure 11.12**). Only lately has You Grow Girl added banner advertising, thus introducing a "revenue stream" and allowing me to classify the site as commercial. Whatever its classification, the mood of the site still remains "home-grown" (if you'll excuse the fruitful pun).

You Grow Girl has attracted a community of gardening enthusiasts due in part to its fun and unique design. On some pages, **yougrowgirl.com** has an almost antique feel, often incorporating hand-drawn botanical illustrations of seeds and plants into its design.

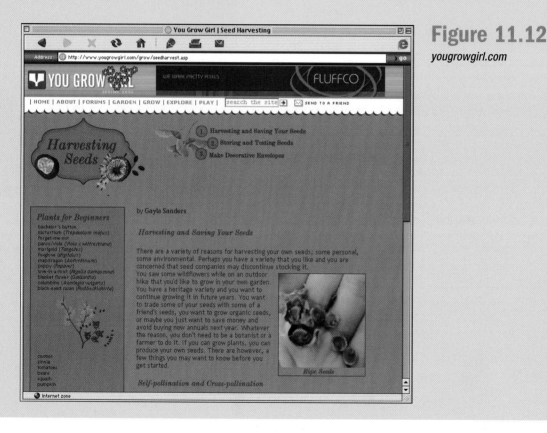

**Figure 11.12**

*yougrowgirl.com*

# Techniques

There is nothing about a site's architecture or layout that makes it inherently 1950s Hello Kitty. Instead, this style is expressed via its graphics. Consequently, 1950s Hello Kitty works equally well in print, as Futurefarmers' print portfolio aptly illustrates.

# Tiny 3D Bubble People/Large 3D Text

I'll go ahead and disappoint you right off the bat. The simple step-by-step method for making smoothly moving 3D Shockwave bubble people is not revealed in this chapter, because it doesn't exist. Many of Futurefarmers' Shockwave files are actually more akin to interactive CD-ROM "games" than they are to web sites proper. The technology itself is no mystery. Futurefarmers uses Illustrator, 3D modeling software, Director, and/or Flash. The characters are drawn, rendered, and animated. It's the particulars of this process that are beyond the scope of this book.

However, some of Franceschini's earlier characters were merely animated gifs, created by rendering the same 3D character in a few different positions and then combining those individual "frames" into a single animated gif. Another lo-fi animation solution is to render a bubble character, save it as a static gif, and then propel it across the screen via the magic of JavaScript-controlled CSS layers (also known as DHTML). Visit **http://hotwired.lycos.com/webmonkey/html/97/31/index2a.html?tw=authoring** for a classic tutorial on how to use DHTML to make stuff zoom around. Or view the source at **http://www.atlasmagazine.com** if you dare.

Fortunately, creating 3D text is simpler than creating Shockwave mini-worlds. You can use 3D modeling software (check the "Techniques" section in Chapter 10, "Drafting Table/Transformer Style," for some options), or you can experiment with a combination of bevels, drop shadows, offset layers, and lighting filters in Photoshop to achieve the desired effect (**Figure 11.13**). Just make sure you start off with a fat, appropriately rounded '50s font.

**Figure 11.13**

*atlastmagazine.com*

# Rounded, Organic Borders

To me, the single distinguishing feature of 1950s Hello Kitty design is its borders. Most web borders consist of lines at 90-degree angles. Occasionally sites implement 45-degree angles or add the odd rounded edges to a content box. In stark contrast to this standard angularity, 1950s Hello Kitty borders are a baroque celebration of organic shapes. They are literally "out of the box." From *Atlas* magazine's frilly swirls (**Figure 11.06**) to You Grow Girl's more symmetrical menu border (**Figure 11.12**), these rounded, organic lines break the monotony of boxy web design.

These rounded borders can be made in Illustrator or Photoshop, depending on how you compose your page. Choose the pen tool and use it to create a path of the shape you desire. Then stroke that path or fill it in, depending on how you intend to use the shape. After you get some organic shapes that you like, you can begin building your own path "library" for use on subsequent projects. Rounded organic shapes have an inordinately strong visual effect on the overall look of any page. Use them wisely.

# Pastel Palettes

Most 1950s Hello Kitty designers use soft, colorful, pastel palettes, but this doesn't automatically mean that your site has to look like a Spice Girls makeup kit. Yes, there is the occasional intense, psycho-happy color scheme (**Figure 11.14**). But there are also more subtle, minimalistic approaches (**Figure 11.09**). Franceschini even manages to pull off what can only be described as pastel greyscale (**Figure 11.08**). Placing transparent colors on top of opaque colors is another color hack that adds dimensionality and "bubbleness" to 1950s Hello Kitty sites (**Figure 11.11**).

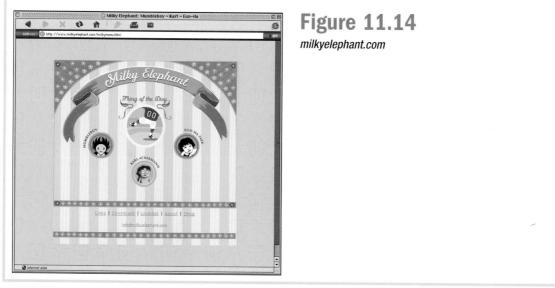

# Figure 11.14

*milkyelephant.com*

# '50s Fonts/'50s Art

Looking at the screenshots in this chapter should give you a pretty good idea of what is meant by '50s fonts. The Avant Card site is a particularly pure example (**Figure 11.11**). They even manage to incorporate some groovy flower-like dingbats and some miniature icons of Saturn. Besides '50s fonts, be on the lookout for some good stock libraries of vintage advertising art. Such embellishments will further enhance your site's mod, retro-kitsch vibe (**Figure 11.15**).

## Figure 11.15
*yougrowgirl.com*

1950s Hello Kitty design is an amalgam of many different influences. Consequently, it can go a lot of directions, from '50s kitsch to psychedelic daydreams of smiling bubble children floating freely above the surface of Planet Cupcake. Obviously, 1950s Hello Kitty design is not for every site. But where applicable, it succeeds magically. And I still think it's the perfect style for yahoo.com. (Jerry Yang, are you reading this?)

# Sites Mentioned in This Chapter

http://www.futurefarmers.com

http://www.yahoo.com

http://www. nutrishnia.org

http://www.atlasmagazine.com

http://www.olivierlaude.com

http://www.posttool.com

http://www.avantcard.com.au

http://www.yougrowgirl.com

http://www.fluffco.com

http://hotwired.lycos.com/
webmonkey/html/97/31/
index2a.html?tw=authoring

http://www.milkyelephant.com

"When I am working on a problem, I never think about beauty... but when I have finished, if the solution is not beautiful, I know it is wrong."

—R. Buckminster Fuller

I'd like to conclude this discourse by offering a defense of graphic design in general, and a defense of graphic design on the web in particular. The main criticism of graphic design is that it is fluff—tangential, nonessential, often doing more harm than good. Yes, we need engineers, and yes, we need usability experts, but why not send the graphic designers packing, along with the hairdressers and copyright lawyers?

What exactly is the purpose of graphic design? Most would say the highest purpose of graphic design (as it relates to interactive/interface design) is to make something easier to use. I agree. But graphic design is also meant to make something enjoyable to use. Can a visit to a web site be both useful *and* enjoyable? Sure. Should it be both? Well, which site will sell more products—a site that is useful and enjoyable, or a site that is merely useful?

Ultimately, a graphic designer is responsible for creating an overall user experience. He translates the purposes and goals of each project into an experience that the user can comprehend, intuit, and feel. Creating usability is *part* of the design process, but it's far from the only part.

# The Cake Decorators Have Become the Carpenters

Graphic design has its obvious benefits in terms of marketing. Put the same exact cola in a Coke bottle and a generic bottle, and most people will say the cola in the Coke bottle tastes better. Graphic design, when used for the purpose of product branding, has the proven ability to alter a user's perception of reality, even when reality itself stays the same. If this type of perception-altering branding were all that graphic design on the web ever accomplished, it would still be worthwhile from a sales perspective. But on the web, where perception *is* reality, graphic design does much more than just create recognizable surface fluff.

On the web, graphic design is not mere icing on some physical real-world product (like cola or aftershave). On the web, graphic design is part of the actual product, because the "product" is often the web site itself. A search engine site is its own product—a piece of software, a tool for parsing data. An e-commerce site is its own product— a piece of software, a tool for instigating and processing commercial transactions. A "virtual" news library, a "virtual" store, a "virtual" community—all these terms describe web sites that are themselves products. When the web is seen in this light, the role of graphic designer changes from superficial to crucial.

To put it more poetically, when the "reality" of a product is virtual rather than physical, graphic designers cease to be the mere "decorators" of the product—they become the "builders" of the product. A print designer who illustrates the exterior of a Happy Meal box is not called a "box builder." And yet a graphic designer who "makes" a web site is called a "site builder." Usability experts are right to be concerned about the havoc a self-indulgent graphic designer can wreak on a web site, because in a very hyper-real sense, graphic design is the "substance" of the web. That is why, on the web more than in any other medium, graphic designers need to know how to communicate effectively.

# It's the Experience, Stupid

If I'm a retailer (particularly a retailer of services), what I'm ultimately offering my customer is an experience. If I'm a boat salesman, my customer isn't just buying a boat; he's buying the potentially enjoyable experiences that boat ownership affords. If I'm a restaurant manager, my patrons aren't just buying food; they're buying an overall dining experience. Likewise, when a customer visits my web site, he's not just coming for the data (contrary to what even he himself might express); he's coming for the experience of finding and absorbing the data. And he's probably coming for even more than that.

Mere subsistence rarely satisfies us humans. We crave an experience in even the most rudimentary tasks. For example, we all need to eat, but we don't all need to eat poached salmon in a white wine sauce. We could just boil our food and eat it—no spices, no sauces, no saute. We could subsist that way. But instead, we've developed countless ways to prepare food. Every culture has its own unique recipes and culinary traditions (**Figure 12.01**). Why?

**Figure 12.01**
*Sushi*

Because (contrary to popular belief) humans are not just smart monkeys. We have souls. We experience things holistically. Good graphic designers are mindful of the soulish aspects of human nature, and they consciously seek to enhance our overall user experience. In one sense, quality design is a celebration of human life. Not content to merely "get by," design takes the necessary machinations of life—driving, purchasing, shopping, learning—and makes those duties not only bearable, but pleasant and enjoyable.

A great designer communicates the following to the person using the object of his design: "Friend, I've been here before you, I've thought about you, and I've worked hard to make your use of this object intuitive and unobjectionable. Beyond that, I've added some extra touches to make your use of this object enjoyable. Celebrate life with me as you use this object, and pass on this same consideration and creativity to others in all you do today."

If all this seems a bit dramatic for "mere" web design, you have yet to envision the web that could be. Return to Chapter 1 and start over. I'll meet you here again on your next pass.

Preserving usability by neutering creative design might be the safest way to "get by," but it sure is boring. We end up settling for unobjectionable communication when we might have achieved excellent communication. How much better to employ creative design in the service of usability! Our users will have an experience one way or another. Will their experience be bland and passable, or will it be delicious and astounding?

## Figure 12.02
*Groovy inflatable plastic chair*

# The Web Is Like a Party

David Siegel famously observed that designing a web site is like designing a display booth for a trade show. You need to present your product in a memorable way, because tons of other people all around you are presenting their products too. Potential customers browse by, and you have only a few seconds to catch their attention and convince them to turn into your booth before they move on to your competitor's booth. (Very insightful, that David Siegel.)

At the last trade show I attended, the most popular booth was the iSyndicate booth. They were throwing colored balls at each other and lounging around in these groovy inflatable plastic chairs (**Figure 12.02**). There were still people standing around holding pamphlets, discussing what they were supposed to be discussing. Commercial promotion was occurring. My wife and daughter immediately wanted to check out the booth with the cool chairs. So did everybody else at the trade show.

What the iSyndicate folks had done was turn their trade show booth into a party. And as I began pondering this, it hit me: *Building a web site is like hosting a party.*

I'm no Martha Stewart, but I do know two classic ways for a host to ruin any party. The first way is overpreparation. A control-freak host can be so concerned about avoiding awkward silences that she leaves no room for spontaneity or serendipity. Every activity is scheduled to the minute, and her guests leave feeling exhausted, never having really gotten a chance to relax or have a casual conversation.

The second classic way for a host to ruin a party is underpreparation. What if you and your date show up at a party and knock on the door, only to be greeted by no one? Upon letting yourselves in, you discover your host, sitting around in his underwear drinking beer and watching *Gilligan's Island* reruns.

He looks up and says, "Hey, wazzup? There should be some leftover pizza in the fridge and some clean dishes in the dishwasher. At least I think they're clean. Just help yourselves. I'll be over here if you need me." Woo-hoo! Some party!

Quality party hosting involves a delicate balance of preparation and spontaneity. It has less to do with what snacks you serve and more to do with the environment you create. You might even say that the key to hosting a great party is being able to create an enjoyable guest *experience*.

And how does all this party analogizing relate to the 10 styles in this book? So glad you asked. Some parties are elegant; other parties are casual. Some parties are wild; other parties are mellow. No single party-hosting style is perfectly suitable for every party. At a fancy party, paper plates won't do. At a cookout, fine china won't do. You can host the most exquisite gourmet meal in the world, but if it's for your rugby mates, they'll probably just wish they were down the road at the local pub having a brew. You can throw the grooviest, trance-a-delic rave in the world, but if it's for your grandparents, all that money you spent on DJ Fresh Kooky will have been for naught.

I have examined 10 fresh design styles that you can use to host your next web party. Only you know who's coming. It's up to you to decide which styles (or combinations thereof) will work best for your particular clambake. Or perhaps these styles will inspire you to develop a radical, heretofore unseen design approach. Wonderful! I'm just trying to act as your friendly web design Martha Stewart. Repulsed at the thought of some dejected designer having to spend his metaphorical Thanksgiving serving up yet another generic web meal at the graphic design equivalent of Denny's, I'm offering some versatile, purpose-specific, home-baked, guest-honoring web design recipes.

So the next time you're tempted to build another bland, passable, generic site, I challenge you to go the extra mile. Discern the heart and soul of the project. Spend some extra time experimenting with an appropriate, project-specific design solution. If your determination flags, remember the innovative web designers in this book, eschewing the conventions of "safe" design to develop a more effective and passionate online design vocabulary. Think of your pitiful site visitor, already bored out of his freaking mind from having to surf the corporate web that Big Brother built. Recall the exhortation of creative muse Willy Wonka, who reminds us that "We are the music makers, and we are the dreamers of the dreams."

For better or worse, the web is literally what we designers make it. So let's make it excellent.

# Index

## Q-R

## T

# NEW RIDERS
# GRAPHICS
# CLASSICS

**Taking Your Talent to the Web**
Jeffrey Zeldman
ISBN: 0735710732
$40.00

**Flash Web Design: the v5 remix**
Hillman Curtis
ISBN: 0735710988
$45.00

**Photoshop 6 Web Magic**
Jeff Foster
ISBN: 0735710368
$45.00

**<designing web graphics.3>**
Lynda Weinman
ISBN: 1562059491
$55.00

**The Art & Science of Web Design**
Jeffrey Veen
ISBN: 0789723700
$45.00

**creative html design.2**
Lynda Weinman and
William Weinman
ISBN: 0735709726
$39.99

**Don't Make Me Think!**
Steve Krug
ISBN: 0789723107
$35.00

The Authors. The Content. The Timeliness.

What it takes to be a classic.

New Riders